THE CHOCOLATE COOKBOOK

THE CHOCOLATE COOKBOOK

ELIZABETH WOLF COHEN

THE
APPLE
PRESS

A QUINTET BOOK

Published by The Apple Press
6 Blundell Street
London N7 9BH

ISBN 1-85076-405-0

This book was designed and produced by
Quintet Publishing Limited
6 Blundell Street
London N7 9BH

Project Editor: Laura Sandelson
Creative Director: Richard Dewing
Designer: Stuart Walden
Editor: Beverly Le Blanc
Photographer: Nelson Hargreaves
Home Economists: Pamela Westland, Suzanne Ardley

Typeset in Great Britain by
Central Southern Typesetters, Eastbourne
Manufactured in Hong Kong by
Regent Publishing Services Limited
Printed in Hong Kong by
Leefung-Asco Printers Limited

ACKNOWLEDGMENT
The publishers would like to thank Cadbury Ltd,
Bournville, England, for supplying chocolate
and cocoa used in the preparation of the recipes.

Table of contents

Introduction

1 Plain chocolate	4 Imported milk chocolate	7 White chocolate
2 Imported plain chocolate	5 Milk chocolate	8 Imported plain chocolate
3 Baker's chocolate (unsweetened)	6 Cocoa	9 Milk chocolate

TYPES OF CHOCOLATE

Chocolate can be found in many forms from solid to premelted, from extra dark to white, from unsweetened to sweet and milky. In its powdered form, chocolate is cocoa powder. All chocolate, even those of the same type, tastes different depending on the quality and roasting of the beans, the quality and style of production and the national tastes of the country in which the chocolate is manufactured.

Both eating and cooking chocolate are made from chocolate liquor, which is blended with additional cocoa butter, sugar and flavourings. The more chocolate liquor and cocoa butter the chocolate contains, the higher the quality. Each country of production has certain minimum standards. Although certain chocolate lends itself to particular preparations, chocolate is very much a personal preference.

PLAIN OR BITTERSWEET CHOCOLATE

This dark type of chocolate varies from bittersweet to the slightly sweeter plain. Bittersweet is not as widely available as plain. This chocolate contains only chocolate liquor, cocoa butter and sometimes lecithin (an emulsifier) and sugar in varying quantities, as well as sometimes vanilla. Each country has varying guidelines for the contents of cocoa solids which accounts for the broad variety of quality. In the UK, this chocolate must contain 35 percent solids, and in the US, 34 percent. Best results in cooking are obtained with chocolate which contains a minimum of 50 percent chocolate solids. Although interchangeable in most of the recipes in this book, the more bitter chocolate is preferable for some of them.

COUVERTURE OR COVERING CHOCOLATE

This is a very fine, richly flavoured chocolate with a glossy appearance and smooth texture because of the high proportion of cocoa butter it contains. It is expensive and mostly used by professionals for coating and dipping other chocolates. This chocolate must be tempered (p8). Although it can be used when a very fine flavour and texture are required, it is not generally used in baking or dessert making.

Do not confuse couverture with commercial coating chocolate or cake covering, made with the addition of other fats and oils, which is cheaper and easier to use but lacks the flavour and gloss of fine couverture.

WHITE CHOCOLATE

Technically, white chocolate is not chocolate at all because it does not contain any chocolate liquor. It is a commercial product made from cocoa butter, milk and sugar. In the US, it is called a confectionery coating, and some white chocolate may contain vegetable fat as well as, or instead of, cocoa butter, so read the label carefully. White chocolate has been gaining in popularity recently and is used in mousses, cakes and sauces, and to contrast in colour with other chocolates. As with milk chocolate, it is more sensitive to heat, so be very careful when melting it. Use a water-bath or "bain marie" and keep the temperature between 44°C/110°F and 48°C/120°F.

UNSWEETENED CHOCOLATE

Also known as Baker's chocolate, or bitter chocolate (not bittersweet), unsweetened chocolate is the cooled chocolate liquor with a quantity of cocoa butter reblended. It has a bitter, intense, full chocolate flavour and is used mainly in manufacturing chocolate products. It is not widely available in the UK but may be found in some specialist shops. An adequate substitution for 25 g/1 oz unsweetened chocolate for baking is 20 g/¾ oz cocoa powder, plus 15 g/½ oz unsalted butter. The sugar in the recipe must then also be adjusted.

CHOCOLATE CHIPS

Originally produced by chocolate manufacturers for use in chocolate chip cookies, these pieces are now available as plain, milk and white. Because they were designed to keep their shape in a variety of baked goods, they are best used in recipes like biscuits, cakes and confections where their shape adds extra texture or interest. Although they can be melted, they contain less cocoa butter than ordinary chocolate.

COCOA POWDER

Cocoa powder is the pure chocolate mass which is left when some of the cocoa butter is removed from the chocolate liquor. Ground and sifted, this powder gives the most intense chocolate flavor to baked goods and desserts.

In baking, cocoa should be sifted into other dry ingredients or diluted with boiling water to form a paste, much like cornstarch, before being added to other mixtures.

Drinking chocolate is a commercial preparation with added sugar and sometimes dried milk solids.

MILK CHOCOLATE

In 1875, Daniel Peter succeeded in adding condensed milk to chocolate liquor which produced the first milk chocolate. Nowadays, milk chocolate is made most commonly with dried milk powder. It has a much milder flavour than dark chocolate and cannot be substituted for bittersweet or dark chocolate in baking and dessert recipes because it has a lower cocoa solid content. Milk chocolate scorches easily when melting, so take care.

COOKING WITH CHOCOLATE

Chocolate must be treated very carefully. The single most important technique to be mastered in cooking with chocolate is melting it. There are several ways to melt chocolate, but there are only a few basic rules to follow for successful results.

If chocolate is being melted on its own, all the equipment and utensils involved must be *perfectly dry*, as even a single drop of water may cause the chocolate to "block," that is, thicken and become a stiff, unworkable paste. For this reason, do not cover the pan at any time during or after melting chocolate. If chocolate does block while being melted alone, try adding a little white vegetable fat (not butter or margarine as these both contain water) and mix well. If this does not work, start again. Do not discard the chocolate, it may be used in a recipe which melts the chocolate in another liquid.

Chocolate can be melted with a liquid, if there is enough liquid. If melted with butter, cream, milk, water, coffee or a liqueur, it is less likely to burn. Generally 15 ml/1 tbsp liquid to 50 g/2 oz chocolate should be safe, but if the chocolate appears to be thickening, add a little more liquid.

With or without liquid, chocolate should be melted *very slowly*. It is very easily burned or scorched, and overheated chocolate can turn gritty and develop a poor flavour. Whatever the method used, chocolate should not be heated above 48°C/120°F; milk and white chocolate should not be heated above 44°C/110°F. Remember this will feel *warm* not hot as normal body temperature is 38°C/98.6°F. If chocolate is broken up into small pieces it will melt smoothly and quickly.

DOUBLE BOILER METHOD

This is probably the most traditional method for melting chocolate. If you do not have a double boiler, create one by placing a small heatproof bowl over a saucepan. Make sure the bowl fits snugly so none of the water or steam can splash into the bowl. Leave the water in the bottom of the double boiler or pan to come to the boil, then place the chocolate, broken into small pieces or chopped, into the double boiler top or bowl and place on double boiler bottom or saucepan. Lower the heat or turn it off completely and allow the chocolate to melt slowly, stirring frequently until smooth.

SAUCEPAN METHOD (DIRECT HEAT)

When chocolate is melted with a liquid such as milk, cream or even butter, it can be melted over direct heat in a saucepan. Choose a heavy-bottomed saucepan and melt the chocolate over low heat, stirring frequently until it is melted and smooth. Remove from heat immediately. This method is also used for making sauces, frostings and some candies.

Chocolate can also be melted in a very low oven (110°C/22°F/Gas Mark ¼ or less). Place the chocolate in the oven for a few minutes. Remove the chocolate before it is completely melted and stir until smooth.

MICROWAVE METHOD

The microwave is perfect for melting chocolate quickly and easily. The chopped or broken chocolate should be placed in a microwave-safe bowl and cooked on Medium power (50%) about 2 minutes for 100g /4 oz plain or bittersweet chocolate. Milk and white chocolate should be melted on Low power (30%) for about 3 minutes for 100 g/4 oz chocolate. (These times are for a 650w–700w oven.) These are *approximate* times and both chocolate and microwave ovens vary, so check the chocolate halfway through cooking time. The chocolate does not change shape, but begins to look shiny and must then be stirred until melted and smooth. *Take care;* chocolate can burn in the microwave so be sure to check frequently and continue to microwave at 5- to 10-second intervals if chocolate is not melted enough.

Chocolate melted with liquid or butter may melt more quickly if the liquid has a high-fat content, so check the time carefully.

TEMPERING CHOCOLATE

Tempering is a process of slowly heating and cooling chocolate to stabilize the emulsification of cocoa solids and butter fat. This technique is generally used by professionals with couverture chocolate, which allows chocolate to shrink quickly (for easy release from a mould) or to be kept at room temperature for several weeks or months without loosing its crispness and shiny surface. All solid chocolate is tempered in production, but once melted it loses its "temper" and must be re-tempered unless it is to be used immediately.

Untempered chocolate tends to "bloom," that is, becomes dull and streaky or takes on a cloudy appearance, but this can be avoided if melted chocolate is refrigerated immediately. General baking and dessert making does not require tempering, which is a relatively fiddly procedure and takes practice and experience. It is, however, used to prepare the chocolate before making many sophisticated decorations such as Chocolate Curls and Scrolls (see Decorating in Chocolate). These shapes and decorations can easily be made without tempering chocolate if they are refrigerated immediately and stored in the refrigerator. Basically, chilling the chocolate solidifies the cocoa butter and prevents it from rising to the surface or "blooming."

Couverture chocolate is usually used for coating because its high butterfat content means it melts to a fluid and beautiful coating consistency. Tempering requires a thermometer. Melt the chocolate in the top of a double boiler by heating it to 38–46°C/100–115°F, stirring frequently. Remove the top of the double boiler and set in a pan or bowl of cold water to cool chocolate to 26°C/80–82°F, stirring constantly. Return the top of the double boiler to the heat and reheat the chocolate to 30–34°C/86–91°F for dark chocolates, from 29–30°C/84–88°F

for milk chocolate and from 29–30°C/84–86°F for white chocolate. The chocolate must be maintained at this temperature, setting the double boiler top in a bowl of warm water or on a heating pad. Any leftover chocolate can be used again but if melted down, will require tempering.

CHOCOLATE FOR COATING

Truffles, caramels and other sweets, as well as fresh or dried fruit pieces, can all be coated in chocolate. The tempered couverture chocolate described above is the ideal method, but melted bittersweet or plain chocolate can be used if the chocolate is refrigerated immediately.

Melt the chocolate by the preferred method, then pour into a bowl deep enough to cover whatever is being coated. The temperature should be between 44 and 48°C/110 and 120°F but never above that. Use a fondue fork, skewer or special chocolate dipping fork to lower the sweet into the chocolate. Turn to coat, and lift out of the melted chocolate, tapping gently on the edge of the bowl to remove excess chocolate. Place on a waxed paper-lined baking sheet, and, if you like, draw tines of fork across the top, to leave two raised ridges.

MOULDING CHOCOLATE

Making Easter eggs and chocolate bunnies or Santas is easy to do at home. There are many especially shaped moulds available in metal and plastic; plastic is easier to use and allows the beginner to see when the chocolate has set and shrunk. The moulds must be immaculately clean; do not use abrasive materials to clean any mould as even the slightest scratch may cause the chocolate to stick.

Melt and temper couverture or bittersweet or plain chocolate as described above (large moulds may need several layers of chocolate), and pour into the mould, tilting the mould and swirling the chocolate so the mould is completely coated; turn out any excess chocolate. Place mould upside down on a waxed paper-lined baking sheet and allow to set until firm. Repeat if necessary and then allow chocolate to set until hard and chocolate begins to shrink away from the edge of the mould. Gently shake the shape out of the mould, without touching it (this would leave fingerprints) onto waxed paper. Use melted chocolate as "glue" to stick together two halves of shapes like Easter eggs and other figures. Tie larger moulds with ribbon or decorate with white icing to give as presents.

DECORATING WITH CHOCOLATE

Chocolate makes an ideal decoration for most desserts and cakes, even those which are not made with chocolate. Some are very simple to make, while others require more skill and patience. It is worth making most chocolate decorations in quantity, as they can be stored for several weeks in an airtight container in the refrigerator depending on whether the chocolate is tempered or not (see page 8).

GRATED CHOCOLATE

Chill the chocolate and hold it with a piece of foil to prevent the heat of your hand melting it. Hold a hand or box grater over a large bowl and grate the amount of chocolate required. A food processor fitted with the metal blade can also be used to grate chocolate, *but* be sure the chocolate is soft enough to be pierced with a sharp knife. Cut the chocolate into small pieces and with the machine running, drop the chocolate pieces through the feed tube until grated (this produces very fine shavings).

EASY CHOCOLATE CURLS

Bring a thick piece or bar of chocolate to room temperature (too cold the chocolate will "grate" and too warm it will slice). With a swivel-bladed vegetable peeler held over a baking sheet or plate, draw the blade along the edge of the chocolate, letting curls fall onto the baking sheet in a single layer. Use a skewer or cocktail stick to transfer them to the dessert or cake because your fingers will melt the curls.

LONG CHOCOLATE CURLS

These curls are best made with dark chocolate which is melted with white vegetable fat (about 5 ml/25 g/1 oz chocolate keeps the chocolate slightly malleable). Melt 175 g/6 oz bittersweet or plain chocolate with 30 ml/2 tbsp white vegetable fat, stirring until smooth. Pour into a small, foil-lined rectangular or square tin to produce a 2.5 cm/1 in thick block. Refrigerate until set. Leave the block to come to room temperature. Use a box grater to produce long curls or a swivel-bladed vegetable peeler for shorter rounder curls.

SCROLLS OR SHORT ROUND CURLS

Melted dark or white chocolate, tempered chocolate or chocolate prepared for Long Chocolate Curls (above) can be used to produce these scrolls. Prepare the melted chocolate and pour onto a marble slab or onto the back of a baking sheet; with a palette knife, spread to about 3 mm/1/8 in thick and leave to set until firm, about 30 minutes.

To make long scrolls, use the blade of a long, sharp knife on the surface of the chocolate and both hands to push away from your body at a 45° angle to scrape off a thin layer of chocolate. Twist the handle of the knife one-quarter of a circle to produce a slightly cone-shaped scroll. To make shorter round curls with a rounder shape, use a teaspoon to scrape chocolate away.

A variety of shapes and sizes can be produced, depending on the temperature of the chocolate and the utensil used to scrape the chocolate into curls. Knives, palette knives, paint scrapers, teaspoons, tablespoons and even wide, straight, pastry scrapers can be used. The colder the chocolate the more it will splinter; warmer chocolate gives a softer looser curl, but do not let the chocolate become too soft or warm or it will be too difficult to handle or may begin to bloom.

A marbled effect can be achieved by pouring about 25 g/1 oz melted chocolate of a contrasting colour over the back of a baking sheet in a swirling pattern, then pouring over the melted chocolate of the main colour and spreading it as directed. When scraped off it will have a marbled effect.

CHOCOLATE SHAPES

Prepare melted chocolate, but pour onto a waxed paper-lined baking sheet and spread evenly to about 3 mm/⅛ in thick. Leave to cool until firm, at least 30 minutes. Invert the chocolate onto another sheet of waxed paper and, with a knife, trim edges to make a perfect rectangle. Using a ruler, mark even squares, rectangles or diamond shapes and then cut out with a knife. Alternatively, use biscuit cutters or aspic cutters to make decorative shapes. Use a plain pastry nozzle to punch a hole in the top and thread with a ribbon for ornaments or use a contrasting chocolate to decorate with another design or write names on the surface.

A marbled effect can be achieved by swirling in a small amount of a contrasting chocolate colour (about 25 g/1 oz to 175 g/6 oz) to the main colour and allowing it to set before cutting out shapes.

CHOCOLATE LEAVES

Any fresh, non-toxic leaf with distinct veins, such as rose, bay or lemon leaves, can be used. Wash and dry leaves thoroughly. Melt the chocolate and use a pastry brush or spoon to completely coat each veined side of leaf. Place coated leaves chocolate-side up on a waxed paper-lined baking sheet to set. Starting at the stem end, gently peel away leaf and return chocolate leaves to waxed paper until ready to use.

DRIZZLED CHOCOLATE

Melt chocolate and spoon into a paper cone (see below) or small piping bag fitted with a very small plain nozzle. Drizzle chocolate onto a waxed paper-lined baking sheet in small, self-contained lattice shapes, such as circles or squares, then leave to set until firm, about 30 minutes, before peeling off paper.

Chocolate can be piped in many designs, such as flowers or butterflies. Place a sheet of waxed paper over a chosen design and pipe chocolate, tracing over the design or shape as a guide. Pull paper over design for each tracing.

For butterflies, pipe chocolate onto individually cut squares and leave until just beginning to set. Use an egg carton or empty box of foil or plastic wrap and place the butterfly shapes between the cups or onto box so it is bent in the centre, creating the butterfly shape. Chill until ready to use.

CHOCOLATE CUPS

Bun or sweet paper cases can be used to make small or mini-chocolate cases to fill with ice creams, mousses, puddings or other dessert mixtures. Use double cases inside each other for extra support. Melt dark, milk or white chocolate and, using a spoon or pastry brush, completely coat the bottom and sides of the case. Leave to set, then add a second layer of melted chocolate. Leave to set overnight or at least 5 to 6 hours. Carefully peel off paper case.

MAKING A PAPER CONE

A paper cone is ideal for piping small amounts of messy liquids like melted chocolate because they are small and easy to handle and can be thrown away; this avoids cleaning a paper bag. Fold a square of greaseproof paper or parchment paper in half to form a triangle. With triangle point facing you, fold left corner down to centre. Fold right corner down and wrap completely around folded left corner, forming a cone. Fold ends into cone. Spoon liquid into cone and fold top edges over to enclose filling. When ready to pipe, snip off end of point to make a hole about 3 mm/⅛ in in diameter.

Cakes

CLASSIC DEVIL'S FOOD CAKE

CHOCOLATE CHESTNUT ROULADE

CHOCOLATE ANGEL CAKE

MARBLED CHOCOLATE AND PEANUT BUTTER BUNDT CAKE

CHOCOLATE SOURED CREAM CAKE

SAUCY CHOCOLATE CAKE

CHOCOLATE-MINT CUP CAKES

CHOCOLATE PECAN TORTE

WHITE CHOCOLATE AND COCONUT LAYER CAKE

EASY CHOCOLATE TRUFFLE CAKE

BLACKOUT CAKE

CHOCOLATE AND RASPBERRY TORTE

BLACK FOREST GATEAU

CHOCOLATE AND BANANA SWIRL CHEESECAKE

WHITE CHOCOLATE CHEESECAKE

TRIPLE CHOCOLATE CHEESECAKE

CLASSIC DEVIL'S FOOD CAKE

10–12 SERVINGS

This is a rich, dark chocolate layer cake with a reddish tint which comes from the cocoa powder. It is filled and iced with a smooth chocolate ganache icing – a chocolate lover's dream cake.

50 g/2 oz plain chocolate, chopped
65 g/2½ oz cocoa powder
250 g/9 oz light plain flour
10 ml/2 tsp bicarbonate of soda
2.5 ml/½ tsp salt
150 g/5 oz unsalted butter, softened
425 g/15 oz soft brown sugar
15 ml/1 tbsp vanilla essence
3 eggs
175 ml/6 fl oz soured cream
5 ml/1 tsp vinegar
250 ml/8 fl oz boiling water

CHOCOLATE GANACHE ICING
675 ml/24 fl oz whipping cream
675 g/1½ lbs plain chocolate, chopped
15 ml/1 tbsp vanilla essence

Preheat oven to 190°C/375°F/Gas Mark 5. Butter two 23 cm/9 in round cake tins, 4 cm/1½ in deep. Line bottoms with waxed paper; butter paper and flour tins.

In the top of a double boiler over low heat, melt chocolate, stirring frequently until smooth. Set aside. Sift together cocoa powder, flour, bicarbonate of soda and salt.

With electric mixer, cream butter, brown sugar and vanilla until light and creamy, about 5 minutes, scraping side of bowl occasionally. Add eggs, 1 at a time, beating well after each addition.

Add flour mixture alternately with soured cream in 3 batches, beating until well blended. Stir in vinegar and slowly beat in boiling water; batter will be thin. Pour into tins.

Bake 20–25 minutes, until a fine skewer inserted in centre comes out with just a few crumbs attached. Cool cakes in tins on wire rack. Remove cakes from tins. Remove from paper and cool on wire rack while preparing icing.

In a saucepan over medium heat, bring cream to the boil. Remove from heat and stir in chocolate all at once until melted and smooth. Cool slightly. Pour into large bowl and refrigerate 1 hour, stirring twice, until icing is spreadable.

With serrated knife, slice each cake layer horizontally into 2 layers. Place 1 cake layer cut-side up on cake plate and spread with one-sixth of the icing. Place second layer on top and cover with another sixth of the icing. Place a third layer on top and cover with another sixth of the icing, then cover with fourth cake layer top-side (rounded) up. Ice top and sides of cake with remaining icing. Serve at room temperature.

SWEET SUCCESS

Cake layers can be made several days ahead, wrapped tightly in plastic wrap and stored in the refrigerator. Bring to room temperature before icing. Ganache icing should be used when it reaches spreading consistency.

CAKES

CHOCOLATE-CHESTNUT ROULADE

12 SERVINGS

This combination of a dark chocolate sponge and chestnut flavoured cream is an elegant one.

175 g/6 oz plain chocolate, chopped
120 ml/4 fl oz strong coffee
6 eggs, separated
90 ml/6 tbsp caster sugar
2.5 ml/½ tsp cream of tartar
10 ml/2 tsp vanilla essence
cocoa powder for dusting

CHESTNUT CREAM FILLING
450 ml/16 fl oz double cream
30 ml/2 tbsp coffee-flavoured liqueur
   or 10 ml/2 tsp vanilla essence
475 ml/16 fl oz canned sweetened
   chestnut purée
icing sugar
chopped marrons for decoration

Preheat oven to 180°C/350°F/Gas Mark 4. Grease bottom and sides of 38.75 × 26 × 2.5 cm/15½ × 10½ × 1 in Swiss roll tin. Line bottom with waxed paper, allowing 2.5 cm/1 in overhang; grease and flour paper.

In the top of a double boiler over low heat, melt chocolate with coffee, stirring frequently until smooth. Set aside.

With an electric mixer, beat egg yolks with half the sugar until pale and thick, about 5 minutes. Slowly beat in chocolate just until blended.

In another large bowl with electric mixer, beat egg whites and cream of tartar until stiff peaks form. Gradually sprinkle sugar over whites in 2 batches and continue beating until whites are stiff and glossy; beat in vanilla.

Stir 1 spoonful of whites into chocolate mixture to lighten, then fold in remaining whites. Spoon into prepared tin, spreading evenly.

Bake 12–15 minutes, or until cake springs back when touched with fingertip.

Meanwhile, dust tea towel with cocoa powder. When cake is done, turn out onto towel immediately and remove paper. Starting at a narrow end, roll cake and towel together Swiss-roll fashion. Cool completely.

With electric mixer, whip cream and liqueur until soft peaks form. Beat 1 spoonful of cream into chestnut purée to lighten, then fold in remaining cream.

Unroll roulade and trim edges. Spread chestnut cream mixture to within 2.5 cm/1 in of edge of cake. Using the towel to lift the cake, roll cake.

Place roulade seam-side down on a serving plate. Decorate the roulade with bands of sifted icing sugar and chopped marrons.

CHOCOLATE ANGEL CAKE

This cake contains absolutely no fat at all and can be eaten plain, drizzled with a raspberry purée, chocolate syrup or chocolate sauce. I top it with an angel light Chocolate Whipped Cream.

200 g/7 oz icing sugar
100 g/4 oz light plain flour
40 g/1½ oz cocoa powder
12 egg whites
7.5 ml/1½ tsp cream of tartar
7.5 ml/1½ tsp vanilla essence
200 g/7 oz caster sugar

CHOCOLATE WHIPPED CREAM
75 g/3 oz plain chocolate chips
300 ml/10 fl oz whipping cream
15 ml/1 tbsp caster sugar

Preheat oven to 180°C/350°F/Gas Mark 4.

Into a bowl sift together icing sugar, flour and cocoa powder; set aside.

In another bowl with electric mixer, beat egg whites, cream of tartar and vanilla until stiff peaks form. Gradually sprinkle in caster sugar, 30 ml/2 tbsp at a time, beating well after each addition, until whites are stiff and glossy. Sprinkle flour mixture over and gently fold in just until blended. Gently spoon into *ungreased* 25 cm/10 in angel cake or tube tin, spreading evenly.

Bake 35–40 minutes, or until cake springs back when lightly touched with fingertip. Immediately invert cake in tin onto a funnel or bottle to cool completely.

With knife or palette knife, loosen cake from tin and place on plate.

Prepare whipped cream. In a saucepan over low heat, melt half the chocolate chips with 75 ml/2½ fl oz cream, stirring until smooth; set aside to cool.

With electric mixer, whip remaining cream with caster sugar until soft peaks form. Fold 1 spoonful of whipped cream into chocolate mixture to lighten, then quickly fold chocolate mixture into re-maining cream. Spread on top of cake in a swirling pattern. Sprinkle the remaining chocolate chips over the top of cake.

MARBLED CHOCOLATE AND PEANUT BUTTER BUNDT CAKE

12–14 SERVINGS

This is a moist, buttery cake which combines chocolate and peanut butter, a classic combination.

100 g/4 oz plain chocolate, chopped
225 g/8 oz butter, softened
225 g/8 oz smooth peanut butter
200 g/7 oz sugar
5 eggs
225 g/8 oz plain flour
10 ml/2 tsp baking powder
2.5 ml/½ tsp salt
120 ml/4 fl oz milk

CHOCOLATE PEANUT BUTTER GLAZE
25 g/1 oz butter, cut up
15 ml/1 tbsp smooth peanut butter
45 ml/3 tbsp golden syrup
30 ml/2 tbsp water
5 ml/1 tsp vanilla essence
175 g/6 oz plain chocolate

Preheat oven to 180°C/350°F/Gas Mark 4. Generously grease and flour a 3 litre/pt Bundt tin or 25 cm/10 in tube tin.

In the top of a double boiler over low heat, melt chocolate.

With electric mixer, beat butter, peanut butter and sugar until light and creamy, about 5 minutes, scraping side of bowl occasionally. Add eggs, 1 at a time, beating well after each addition.

In another bowl, stir together flour, baking powder and salt. Add to peanut-butter mixture alternately with milk just until blended.

Pour half the batter into another bowl. Stir melted chocolate into one half until well blended.

Using a large spoon, drop alternate spoonfuls of chocolate batter and peanut-butter batter into the bundt tin.

Using a knife, pull through the batters to create a marbled effect; do not touch side or bottom of tin or over-mix.

Bake 50–60 minutes, until top of cake springs back when touched with finger-tip. Cool cake in tin on wire rack 10 minutes. Unmould onto rack to cool.

Meanwhile, prepare glaze. In a saucepan, combine all the ingredients. Melt over low heat, stirring until smooth. Cool slightly. When slightly thickened, drizzle glaze over cake allowing it to run down sides.

SWEET SUCCESS

To avoid sticking, grease bundt or fluted pans very generously, especially the ridges, as you cannot use a knife to loosen edge.

MARBLED CHOCOLATE AND PEANUT BUTTER BUNDT CAKE ▶

CHOCOLATE SOURED CREAM CAKE

12–15 SERVINGS

Make the icing while the cake is cooling and pour over the cake while both are warm for a rich, moist result.

100 g/4 oz butter, softened
200 g/7 oz sugar
4 eggs
225 g/8 oz plain flour
50 g/2 oz cocoa powder
15 ml/1 tbsp baking powder
5 ml/1 tsp bicarbonate of soda
250 ml/8 fl oz soured cream
175 g/6 oz chocolate chips

CHOCOLATE SOURED CREAM ICING
250 g/9 oz chocolate, chopped
40 g/1½ oz butter
120 ml/4 fl oz soured cream
5 ml/1 tsp vanilla essence
600 g/1¼ lbs sugar, sifted

Preheat oven to 180°C/350°F/Gas Mark 4. Grease and flour 32.5 × 23 cm/13 × 9 in baking dish or cake tin.

With electric mixer, beat butter and sugar until light and creamy, about 5 minutes, scraping side of bowl occasionally. Add eggs, 1 at a time, beating well after each addition.

In another bowl, sift together flour, cocoa powder, baking powder and bicarbonate of soda. Add to egg mixture alternately with soured cream, beating just until blended; stir in chocolate chips. Pour into prepared dish or tin and spread evenly.

Bake 25–30 minutes, until a fine skewer inserted in centre comes out clean. Cool on wire rack.

Meanwhile, prepare icing. In a saucepan over low heat, melt chocolate and butter, stirring until smooth. Cool about 10 minutes. Stir in soured cream and vanilla.

With wooden spoon, gradually beat in icing sugar until icing is thick and smooth. Pour over warm cake and spread evenly. Cool iced cake completely.

SWEET SUCCESS

If using Chocolate Soured Cream Icing to fill and ice a layer cake or fairy cakes, allow icing to cool completely until spreading consistency.

SAUCY CHOCOLATE CAKE

8 SERVINGS

During baking, the cake batter sets and a creamy, saucy layer settles on the bottom, creating its own sauce.

100 g/4 oz plain flour
90 g/3½ oz sugar
75 ml/5 tbsp cocoa powder
10 ml/2 tsp baking powder
2.5 ml/½ tsp salt
175 ml/6 fl oz milk
25 g/1 oz butter
5 ml/1 tsp vanilla essence

TOPPING
150 g/5 oz light brown sugar
50 g/2 oz chopped pecans (optional)
400 ml/14 fl oz boiling water
icing sugar for dusting

Preheat oven to 180°C/350°F/Gas Mark 4. Lightly butter 20 × 20 × 5 cm/8 × 8 × 2 in baking dish.

Combine flour, sugar, 45 ml/3 tbsp cocoa powder, baking powder and salt. Stir in milk, butter and vanilla just until blended. Spoon into dish and spread evenly.

In another bowl, combine brown sugar, chopped nuts and remaining 30 ml/2 tbsp cocoa; gradually stir in boiling water until sugar dissolves. Gently pour over batter in baking dish.

Bake 25–30 minutes, until top of cake springs back when touched with fingertip. Cool 30–40 minutes on wire rack. Dust with icing sugar and serve warm or chilled.

SWEET SUCCESS

This is an easy cake to prepare and bake at the last minute or when unexpected guests drop in. Most of the ingredients are pantry staples.

CHOCOLATE MINT CUP CAKES

18–20 SERVINGS

These fairy cakes are a moist, dark chocolate cake with a refreshing hint of mint echoed in the Chocolate Mint Glaze. They make an ideal snack for adults and children.

225 g/8 oz light plain flour
5 ml/1 tsp bicarbonate of soda
1.5 ml/¼ tsp salt
50 g/2 oz cocoa powder
150 g/5 oz butter, softened
275 g/10 oz caster sugar
3 eggs
10 ml/2 tsp peppermint essence
225 ml/8 fl oz milk

CHOCOLATE MINT GLAZE
75 g/3 oz plain chocolate
50 g/2 oz butter
5 ml/1 tsp peppermint essence

Preheat oven to 180°C/350°F/Gas Mark 4. Line twenty deep muffin or bun tins with paper cases.

Sift together flour, bicarbonate of soda, salt and cocoa powder.

In a second large bowl with electric mixer, beat butter and sugar until light and creamy, about 5 minutes. Add eggs, 1 at a time, beating well after each addition, then beat in mint essence.

On low speed, beat in flour and cocoa mixture alternately with milk just until blended. Spoon into paper cases filling each tin about three-quarters full.

Bake 12–15 minutes, until a fine skewer inserted in centre, comes out clean; do not overbake. Cool in tins on wire rack 5 minutes; remove cakes to wire rack to cool completely.

Meanwhile, prepare glaze. In a saucepan over low heat, melt chocolate and butter, stirring until smooth. Remove from heat and stir in mint essence. Cool until spreadable, then spread on top of each cake.

CHOCOLATE PECAN TORTE

This European-style torte does not contain any flour, but uses ground pecans instead. Walnuts, hazelnuts or almonds can be substituted. The "cake" is baked in a water-bath to keep it extra moist.

200 g/7 oz plain chocolate, chopped
150 g/5 oz unsalted butter, cut into pieces
4 eggs
100 g/4 oz sugar
10 ml/2 tsp vanilla essence
90 g/3½ oz ground pecans

CHOCOLATE HONEY GLAZE
100 g/4 oz plain chocolate, chopped
50 g/2 oz unsalted butter, cut into pieces
30 ml/2 tbsp honey
24 pecan halves for decoration

Preheat oven to 180°C/350°F/Gas Mark 4. Grease 20 cm/8 in, 5 cm/2 in deep springform tin; line bottom with waxed paper and grease waxed paper. Wrap bottom of tin in foil.

In a saucepan over low heat, melt chocolate and butter, stirring until smooth. Remove from heat.

With electric mixer, beat eggs with sugar and vanilla just until frothy, 1–2 minutes. Stir in melted chocolate and ground nuts until well blended. Pour into tin and tap gently on work surface to break any large air bubbles.

Place tin into larger roasting tin and pour boiling water into roasting tin, about 2 cm/¾ in up the side of springform tin. Bake 25–30 minutes, until edge of cake is set, but centre is still soft. Remove tin from water-bath and remove foil. Cool on wire rack completely.

Meanwhile, prepare pecan halves for decoration. Place pecan halves on baking sheet and bake 10–12 minutes, until just brown, stirring occasionally.

Prepare glaze. In a saucepan over low heat, melt chocolate, butter and honey, stirring until smooth; remove from heat. Carefully dip toasted nuts halfway into glaze and place on waxed paper-lined baking sheet until set. Glaze will have thickened slightly.

Remove side of tin and turn cake onto wire rack placed over baking sheet to catch any drips. Remove tin bottom and paper so bottom of cake is now the top. Pour thickened glaze over cake, tilting rack slightly to spread glaze. If necessary, use palette knife to smooth sides. Arrange nuts around outside edge of torte and leave glaze to set. With palette knife, carefully slide cake onto serving dish.

SWEET SUCCESS

Cake can be baked 2–3 days ahead, wrapped tightly and refrigerated or even frozen. Bring to room temperature before glazing.

WHITE CHOCOLATE AND COCONUT LAYER CAKE

12–16 SERVINGS

Layered and iced with a white chocolate-mousse mixture, then covered with whipped cream and decorated with strips of fresh coconut, this is a delicate white chocolate cake. White crème de cacao could replace the rum.

100 g/4 oz good quality white
   chocolate, chopped
120 ml/4 fl oz whipping cream
120 ml/4 fl oz milk
15 ml/1 tbsp light rum
100 g/4 oz unsalted butter, softened
175 g/6 oz sugar
3 eggs
225 g/8 oz plain flour
5 ml/1 tsp baking powder
pinch salt
75 g/3 oz shredded sweetened coconut

WHITE CHOCOLATE MOUSSE
425 g/15 oz. good quality white
   chocolate, chopped
1 litre/35 fl oz whipping cream
120 ml/4 fl oz light rum
fresh coconut strips for decoration

Preheat oven to 180°C/350°F/Gas Mark 4. Grease and flour 23 cm/9 in round, 5 cm/2 in deep cake tins.

In top of a double boiler over low heat, melt chocolate with cream, stirring until smooth. Stir in milk and rum; set aside to cool.

With electric mixer, beat butter with sugar until pale and thick, about 5 minutes. Add eggs, 1 at a time, beating well after each addition. In another bowl, stir together flour, baking powder and salt. Alternately add flour mixture and melted white chocolate in batches, just until blended; stir in half the coconut. Pour batter into tins and spread evenly.

Bake 20–25 minutes, until a fine skewer inserted in centres comes out clean. Cool on wire rack 10 minutes. Unmould cakes onto wire rack and cool completely.

Meanwhile, prepare mousse. In a saucepan over low heat, melt white chocolate and 350 ml/12 fl oz cream, stirring frequently until smooth. Stir in rum, then pour into bowl. Refrigerate 1–1½ hours, until completely cold and thickened.

Whip remaining cream until soft peaks form. Stir 1 spoonful of cream into mousse mixture to lighten, then fold in about 250 ml/8 fl oz whipped cream.

With serrated knife, slice cake layers in half horizontally, making 4 layers. Place 1 layer on plate and spread one-sixth of mousse on top. Sprinkle with one-third of remaining coconut. Place second layer on top and spread with sixth of mousse. Sprinkle with another third of coconut. Place third layer on top and spread with another sixth of mousse and remaining coconut. Cover with last

cake layer and cover top and sides with remaining mousse.

Spread the remaining whipped cream over top and sides of cake and garnish with fresh coconut strips.

SWEET SUCCESS

If fresh coconut is unavailable, use shredded sweetened coconut for garnish: Spread 40 g/1½ oz coconut on baking sheet and bake at 180°C/ 350°F/Gas Mark 4 10–12 minutes, stirring twice, until golden. Press into sides and sprinkle on top of cake.

For fresh coconut strips, use a swivel-bladed vegetable peeler to make paper-thin strips from fresh coconut pieces. Leave brown skin on pieces to create a pretty edge.

EASY CHOCOLATE TRUFFLE CAKE

16–20 SERVINGS

This must be the most chocolaty, yet easiest, dessert to make. It should be made at least one day before glazing.

250 g/9 oz plain chocolate, chopped
225 g/8 oz unsalted butter, cut into pieces
75 g/3 oz sugar
120 ml/4 fl oz whipping cream
15 ml/1 tbsp vanilla essence
6 eggs

CHOCOLATE GLAZE
175 g/6 oz plain chocolate, chopped
50 g/2 oz butter, cut into pieces
whipped cream for decoration
rose petals

Preheat oven to 180°C/350°F/Gas Mark 4. Generously grease a 23 cm/9 in, 5 cm/2 in deep round or scalloped spring-form tin; line bottom with waxed paper and grease waxed paper. Wrap bottom of tin in foil.

In a saucepan over low heat, melt chocolate, butter and sugar with cream, stirring frequently until smooth; cool slightly. Stir in vanilla.

With electric mixer, beat eggs lightly, about 1 minute. Slowly beat chocolate into eggs until blended. Pour into tin and tap gently on work surface to break any large air bubbles.

Place tin into larger roasting tin and pour boiling water into roasting tin, about 2 cm/¾ in up the sides of spring-form tin. Bake 25–30 minutes, until edge of cake is set, but centre is still soft. Remove tin from water-bath and remove foil. Cool on wire rack com-pletely; cake will sink in centre and may be cracked.

Remove side of tin and turn cake onto wire rack placed over baking sheet to catch any drips. Remove tin bottom and paper.

Prepare glaze. In a saucepan over low heat, melt chocolate and butter, stirring until smooth. Pour over cake, tilting rack slightly to spread glaze. If necessary, use palette knife to smooth side. Leave to set.

With palette knife, carefully slide cake onto serving dish. If you like, pipe whipped cream border around edge. Dip the rose petals in lightly-beaten egg white, then in caster sugar. Allow to stand on greaseproof paper in a cool place for about 2 hours. Place in centre of cake. Serve with softly whipped cream on the side.

EASY CHOCOLATE TRUFFLE CAKE ▶

BLACKOUT CAKE

12–16 SERVINGS

300 g/11 oz plain flour
25 g/1 oz cocoa powder
15 ml/1 tbsp bicarbonate of soda
2.5 ml/½ tsp salt
100 g/4 oz plain chocolate, chopped
175 g/6 oz unsalted butter, softened
350 g/12 oz sugar
3 eggs
10 ml/2 tsp vanilla essence
175 ml/6 fl oz buttermilk
350 ml/12 fl oz strong coffee (boiled)
   or 15 ml/1 tbsp instant coffee
   granules dissolved in 350 ml/12 fl oz
   boiling water

CHOCOLATE GANACHE ICING
300 ml/10 fl oz double cream
450 g/1 lb plain chocolate, chopped
50 g/2 oz butter, cut into pieces
10 ml/2 tsp vanilla essence
grated chocolate for decoration
icing sugar for dusting

Preheat oven to 180°C/350°F/Gas Mark 4. Grease and flour two 23 cm/9 in round, 5 cm/2 in deep cake tins.

Stir together flour, cocoa powder and bicarbonate of soda and salt. In the top of a double boiler over low heat, melt chocolate; set aside.

In a second bowl with electric mixer, beat butter with sugar until light and creamy, about 5 minutes. Add eggs, 1 at a time, beating well after each addition. Beat in chocolate and vanilla.

Add flour mixture to the batter in 2 additions alternately with the butter-milk; beat just until blended. At low speed, slowly beat in boiling coffee until smooth, scraping bowl once; batter will be thin. Pour into prepared tins.

Bake 25–30 minutes, or until a fine skewer inserted in centres comes out with just a few crumbs attached. Cool in tins on wire rack 10 minutes. Unmould and cool completely.

Meanwhile, prepare icing. In a medium saucepan, bring cream to the boil. Remove from heat and immediately stir in chocolate until melted and smooth. Beat in butter and vanilla. Cool; refrigerate 45–55 minutes or until icing is soft but spreadable.

Place 1 cake layer on a plate and cover with one-third of the icing. Place second layer on top and ice top and sides with remaining icing. Press grated chocolate onto sides of cake and sprinkle on top. Dust top with icing sugar.

CHOCOLATE AND RASPBERRY TORTE

10 SERVINGS

A most elegant, delicious torte, ideal for any special occasion. The flavour of chocolate and raspberry is one of my favourites. This can be made without the fresh raspberries, but they add a special touch.

100 g/4 oz plain chocolate, chopped
100 g/4 oz ground blanched almonds
25 g/1 oz plain flour
100 g/4 oz butter, softened
100 g/4 oz sugar
4 eggs, separated
1.5 ml/¼ tsp cream of tartar

CHOCOLATE AND RASPBERRY GANACHE ICING AND FILLING
250 ml/8 fl oz double cream
250 ml/8 fl oz seedless raspberry jam
275 g/10 oz plain chocolate, chopped
25 g/1 oz butter, cut into pieces
60 ml/4 tbsp raspberry-flavour liqueur
225 g/8 oz fresh raspberries, 8 or 10 reserved for decoration
chocolate leaves (see Decorating with Chocolate) for decoration

Preheat oven to 180°C/350°F/Gas Mark 4. Grease bottom and sides of 38.75 × 26 × 2.5 cm/15½ × 10½ × 1 in Swiss roll tin. Line bottom with waxed paper, allowing 2.5 cm/1 in overhang; grease and flour paper.

In the top of a double boiler over low heat, melt chocolate, stirring frequently until smooth. Set aside to cool.

In a bowl, mix ground almonds and flour until blended. In another bowl with electric mixer, beat butter and half the sugar until pale and creamy, about 3 minutes. Add the egg yolks, 1 at a time, beating well after each addition. Slowly beat in melted chocolate until well blended, scraping bowl occasionally.

In a large bowl with electric mixer, beat egg whites with the cream of tartar until stiff peaks form. Gradually sprinkle remaining sugar over whites in 2 batches, beating until whites are stiff and glossy.

Stir 1 spoonful of whites into chocolate mixture to lighten, then fold in remaining whites and almond and flour mixture alternately just until blended. Spoon into tin, spreading evenly.

Bake 10–12 minutes, or until cake springs back when touched with finger-tip.

Cool cake in tin on wire rack 10 minutes. Using paper corners as a guide, lift cake out of tin onto rack to cool completely.

Meanwhile, prepare icing. In a saucepan, bring cream and half the raspberry jam to the boil. Remove from heat and immediately stir in chocolate until melted and smooth. Beat in butter and half the raspberry flavour liqueur. Cool icing mixture, then refrigerate until it reaches a spreading consistency, about 1 hour; stir occasionally.

Turn cake onto work surface, bottom side up. Trim cake edges and cut cake crosswise into 3 equal strips. In a saucepan, melt remaining jam and raspberry flavour liqueur, stirring until smooth; spoon equally over each cake strip and leave to soak in, 2–3 minutes.

Place 1 cake strip on wire rack over a baking sheet to catch drips. Spread with about 250 ml/8 fl oz chilled icing. Sprinkle with half the raspberries. Top with second cake strip and spread with 250 ml/8 fl oz icing and remaining raspberries. Place third cake strip on top, top side up. With palette knife, spread remaining icing over top and sides of torte. Leave to set.

With palette knife, slide cake onto serving dish. Decorate top of torte with chocolate leaves and reserved raspberries.

VARIATION

For a lighter look, beat the frosting with a hand-held beater for 30–45 seconds until light and fluffy. Immediately frost and decorate the torte before the frosting hardens.

BLACK FOREST GATEAU

10 SERVINGS

This classic European cake is based on a cocoa sponge cake. The combination of chocolate, cherries and cream is a delicious one. Try poaching your own fresh cherries in a sugar syrup when they are in season.

65 g/2½ oz light plain flour
40 g/1½ oz cocoa powder
2.5 ml/½ tsp baking powder
5 eggs, separated
200 g/7 oz sugar
1.5 ml/¼ tsp cream of tartar
65 g/2½ oz butter, melted and cooled

CHERRY FILLING
425 g/15 oz can black cherries in juice
    or syrup, stoned
75 ml/5 tbsp cherry flavoured liqueur
30 ml/2 tbsp cornflour, dissolved in
    30 ml/2 tbsp water
475 ml/16 fl oz whipping cream
30 ml/2 tbsp caster sugar
Easy Chocolate Curls (see Decorating
    with Chocolate) for decoration
candied or maraschino cherries for
    garnish

Preheat oven to 180°C/350°F/Gas Mark 4. Grease bottom and sides of 20 cm/ 8 in springform tin. Line bottom with waxed paper; grease paper and flour tin.

Sift together flour, cocoa powder and baking powder; set aside. In a bowl with electric mixer, beat egg yolks with 175 g/6 oz sugar until pale and thick, about 5 minutes.

In another bowl with electric mixer, beat egg whites and cream of tartar until stiff peaks form. Sprinkle in remaining 30 ml/2 tbsp sugar and beat until stiff and glossy.

Stir 1 spoonful of whites into yolk mixture to lighten. Fold in flour and cocoa mixture and remaining egg whites alternately just until blended. Pour melted butter over and fold in just until blended. Spoon into tin spreading evenly.

Bake 30–35 minutes, until a fine skewer inserted in centre comes out clean. Cool in tin on wire rack 10 minutes. Remove side and bottom of tin and cool completely. Peel off paper.

Meanwhile, prepare filling. Drain cherries, reserving juice. Mix 45 ml/ 3 tbsp cherry juice with 45 ml/3 tbsp cherry flavour liqueur; set aside. In a saucepan, stir together remaining cherry juice and cornflour mixture. Bring to the boil, then simmer 2–3 minutes, until thickened. Stir in cherries and set aside to cool.

Whip cream, sugar and remaining cherry flavour liqueur until soft peaks form. Reserve about 120 ml/4 fl oz cream for decoration.

With a serrated knife, cut cake horizontally into 3 layers. Place bottom layer on a plate. Sprinkle over one-third cherry juice syrup and spread with about 350 ml/12 fl oz whipped cream. Spoon half the cherry mixture evenly over cream and cover with second cake layer. Sprinkle third of the cherry juice syrup over and another 350 ml/12 fl oz whipped cream. Spoon remaining cherry mixture over. Sprinkle cut side of third cake layer with remaining cherry juice syrup and place cut side down over cherry layer. Ice top and sides of cake with remaining whipped cream.

Press chocolate curls onto sides of cake. Spoon reserved cream into small piping bag fitted with a medium star nozzle and pipe 10 rosettes evenly around cake. Top each with a candied or maraschino cherry. Refrigerate.

SWEET SUCCESS

Decorate cake with cherries at the last minute to avoid any colour from cherries bleeding into cream.

CHOCOLATE AND BANANA SWIRL CHEESECAKE

16 SERVINGS

I first made this cheesecake in an effort to use some overripe bananas in the kitchen. It uses the flavours of a banana split with hot fudge sauce. The banana mixture is highly perfumed and contrasts with the soft, fudgy chocolate swirls.

CRUMB CRUST
150 g/5 oz ginger snaps
40 g/1½ oz walnuts
50 g/2 oz butter, melted
2.5 ml/½ tsp ground ginger

FILLING
100 g/4 oz plain chocolate, chopped
50 g/2 oz butter, cut into pieces
1 kg/2½ lbs cream cheese, softened
275 g/10 oz sugar
15 ml/1 tbsp vanilla essence
5 eggs
250 ml/8 fl oz soured cream
3 ripe bananas
15 ml/1 tbsp lemon juice

Preheat oven to 180°C/350°F/Gas Mark 4. Lightly grease a 25 cm/10 in, 7.5 cm/3 in deep springform tin.

In a food processor, process ginger snaps and walnuts until fine crumbs form. Pour in melted butter and ginger. Process just until blended. Pat onto bottom and to within 1 cm/½ in of top of sides of tin.

Bake 5–7 minutes, just until set. Remove to wire rack to cool while preparing filling. Lower oven temperature to 150°C/300°F/Gas Mark 2.

In a saucepan over low heat, melt chocolate and butter, stirring frequently until smooth. Set aside to cool.

With electric mixer, beat cream cheese and sugar until smooth, 2–4 minutes; stir in vanilla. Add eggs, 1 at a time, beating well after each addition, scraping bowl occasionally, then blend in soured cream. Pour about 350 ml/12 fl oz of cream cheese mixture into a bowl and stir in melted chocolate until well blended. Set mixture aside.

In a second bowl, mash bananas with lemon juice, then beat into remaining cream cheese mixture until well blended.

Pour banana mixture into baked crust. Drop spoonfuls of chocolate mixture over banana mixture in a circle about 2.5 cm/1 in from sides of tin. With a spoon or knife, swirl chocolate mixture into banana mixture creating a marbled effect. Do not overmix. Place tin on baking sheet; place small saucepan of water on floor of oven to create moisture during baking.

Bake 50–60 minutes, until edge of cheesecake is set, but centre is still soft. Turn off oven and leave to stand 30 minutes; this helps prevent cracking. Transfer to wire rack, run knife around edge of cheesecake in tin to separate it from sides; this also helps prevent cracking. Cool completely, then refrigerate, loosely covered, overnight.

To serve, run knife around edge of tin to loosen cheesecake. Remove side of tin. If you like, slide knife under crust to separate cheesecake from bottom, then, with palette knife, slide onto serving plate. Alternatively, leave cheesecake on tin bottom to avoid breaking crust or surface and serve from tin bottom.

WHITE CHOCOLATE CHEESECAKE

16 – 20 SERVINGS

White chocolate seems the perfect marriage with a cream cheese filling. This rich, creamy cake is based on my classic New York-style cheesecake, but has a more elegant European look!

CRUMB CRUST
150 g/5 oz digestive biscuits
25 g/1 oz pecan or walnut halves
50 g/2 oz butter, melted
2.5 ml/½ tsp ground cinnamon

FILLING
350 g/12 oz good quality white chocolate, chopped
120 ml/4 fl oz whipping cream
675 g/1½ lbs cream cheese
75 g/3 oz sugar
4 eggs
15 ml/1 tbsp vanilla essence
cocoa powder for dusting (optional)
White and Dark Chocolate Curls (see Decorating with Chocolate) for decoration

SOURED CREAM TOPPING
400 ml/14 fl oz soured cream
50 g/2 oz sugar
5 ml/1 tsp vanilla essence

Preheat oven to 180°C/350°F/Gas Mark 4. Lightly grease a 23 cm/9 in, 7.5 cm/in deep springform tin.

Prepare crust. In a food processor, process biscuits and pecans until fine crumbs form. Pour in melted butter and cinnamon. Process just until blended. Pat onto bottom and to within 1 cm/½ in of top of sides of tin.

Bake 5–7 minutes, just until set. Remove to wire rack to cool while preparing filling. Lower oven temperature to 150°C/300°F/Gas Mark 2.

In a saucepan over low heat, melt chocolate with cream, stirring frequently until smooth. Set aside to cool.

With electric mixer, beat cream cheese and sugar until smooth, 2–4 minutes. Add eggs, 1 at a time, beating well after each addition, scraping bowl occasionally. Slowly beat in white-chocolate mixture and vanilla just until blended. Pour into baked crust. Place on baking sheet; place small saucepan of water on floor of oven to create moisture during baking.

Bake 45–55 minutes, or until edge of cheesecake is firm but centre is still slightly soft. Remove cheesecake to wire rack while preparing topping. Increase oven temperature to 200°C/400°F/Gas Mark 6.

In a bowl, beat soured cream, sugar and vanilla. Pour over cheesecake and return to oven. Bake 5 minutes longer. Transfer to wire rack to cool to room temperature. Run knife around edge of cake in tin to separate it from side; this helps prevent cracking. Cool completely, then refrigerate overnight.

To serve, run knife around edge of tin to loosen cheesecake. Remove side of tin. If you like, slide knife under crust to separate cheesecake from bottom, then, with palette knife, slide onto serving plate. Alternatively, leave cheesecake on tin bottom to avoid breaking crust or surface and serve from tin bottom.

Dust top of cheesecake with cocoa or decorate with white and dark chocolate curls.

SWEET SUCCESS

Use back of spoon to press crumbs to bottom and sides of tin.

CAKES

TRIPLE CHOCOLATE CHEESECAKE

This is a very rich, deep chocolate cheesecake surrounded by a chocolate crust, then topped with a chocolate glaze and cocoa finish.

225 g/8 oz plain chocolate digestive biscuits
50 g/2 oz butter, melted
2.5 ml/½ tsp ground cinnamon

FILLING
450 g/1 lb plain chocolate, chopped
50 g/2 oz butter, cut into pieces
250 ml/8 fl oz soured cream
900 g/2 lb cream cheese, softened
225 g/8 oz sugar
5 eggs
15 ml/1 tbsp vanilla essence

CHOCOLATE GLAZE
100 g/4 oz plain chocolate, chopped
120 ml/4 fl oz double cream
5 ml/1 tsp vanilla essence
cocoa powder

Preheat oven to 180°C/350°F/Gas Mark 4. Lightly grease bottom and sides of 25 cm/10 in, 7.5 cm/3 in deep springform tin.

Prepare crust. In a food processor, process chocolate biscuits until fine crumbs form. Pour in melted butter and cinnamon. Process just until blended. Pat onto bottom and to within 1 cm/½ in of top of sides of tin.

Bake 5–7 minutes, just until set. Remove to wire rack to cool while preparing filling. Lower oven temperature to 170°C/325°F/Gas Mark 3.

In a saucepan over low heat, melt chocolate and butter, stirring frequently until smooth. Set aside to cool; stir in soured cream.

With electric mixer, beat cream cheese and sugar until smooth, 2–4 minutes. Add eggs, 1 at a time, beating well after each addition, scraping bowl occasionally. Slowly beat in chocolate mixture and vanilla just until blended. Pour into baked crust. Place tin on baking sheet; place small saucepan of water on floor of oven to create moisture.

Bake 1–1½ hours, or until edge of cheesecake is set but centre is still slightly soft. Turn off the oven but leave cheesecake in the oven for another 30 minutes. Remove to wire rack to cool. Run knife around edge of cheesecake in tin to separate it from side; this helps prevent cracking. Cool to room temperature.

Prepare glaze. In a saucepan, melt chocolate with cream and vanilla, stirring until smooth. Cool and leave to thicken slightly, 10–15 minutes. Pour over warm cake in tin; cool glazed cake completely. Using strips of waxed paper dust cocoa in horizontal bands across the top of the cake. Refrigerate, loosely covered, overnight.

To serve, run knife around edge of tin to loosen cheesecake. Remove side of tin. If you like, slide knife under crust to separate cheesecake from bottom, and, with palette knife, slide onto serving plate. Alternatively, leave cheesecake on tin bottom to avoid breaking crust or surface and serve from tin bottom.

Pies and Pastries

ANTOINE'S CHOCOLATE AND PINE NUT TART

CHOCOLATE AND PECAN PIE

CHOCOLATE CREAM PIE

WHITE CHOCOLATE AND BANANA CREAM TART

MOCHA-FUDGE PIE WITH ESPRESSO CUSTARD CREAM

CHOCOLATE TRUFFLE TART

WHITE CHOCOLATE MOUSSE AND STRAWBERRY TART

CHOCOLATE-CHOCOLATE CREAM PUFFS

DOUBLE-CHOCOLATE BERRY TART
WITH BLACKBERRY SAUCE

BLACK-BOTTOM LEMON TARTLETS

ANTOINE'S CHOCOLATE AND PINE NUT TART

7-8 SERVINGS

My friend Antoine Bouterin, the chef at Le Perigord in New York City, taught me how to make this tart when we toured the U.S. giving cooking demonstrations. I never forgot the combination of warm chocolate, toasted pine nuts and orange zest in a creamy custard – simple, but sometimes the simplest things are best. This is my variation.

SWEET FRENCH TART PASTRY
175 g/6 oz plain flour
50 g/2 oz caster sugar
1.5 ml/¼ tsp salt
100 g/4 oz butter, cut into small pieces
3 egg yolks, lightly beaten
15-30 ml/1–2 tbsp iced water

FILLING
2 eggs
75 g/3 oz sugar
grated zest of 1 orange
15 ml/1 tbsp orange-flavoured liqueur
250 ml/8 fl oz whipping cream
100 g/4 oz plain chocolate, chopped
65 g/2½ oz pine nuts, toasted

GLAZE
1 orange
120 ml/4 fl oz water
50 g/2 oz sugar

Prepare pastry. In a food processor fitted with metal blade, process flour, sugar and salt to blend. Add butter and process 15–20 seconds, until mixture resembles coarse crumbs. Add egg yolks and using *pulse action*, process just until dough begins to stick together; *do not allow dough to form a ball* or pastry will be tough. If dough appears dry, add 15-30 ml/1-2 tbsp iced water, little by little, just until dough holds together.

Turn dough onto lightly floured work surface and using a pastry scraper to scrape dough, knead gently until well blended. Shape dough into flat disc and wrap tightly in plastic wrap. Refrigerate 4–5 hours.

Lightly butter a 23 cm/9 in, 4 cm/1½ in deep tart tin with removable bottom. Soften dough 5–10 minutes at room temperature. On a well-floured surface, roll out dough into a 27.5 cm/11 in circle about 0.5 cm/¼ in thick. Roll dough loosely around rolling pin and unroll over tart tin; ease dough into tin.

With floured fingers, press overhang down slightly toward centre, making top edge thicker, then roll rolling pin over tin edge to cut off excess dough. Press thicker top edge against side of tin to form rim about 0.5 cm/¼ in higher than tin. Using thumb and forefinger, crimp edge. Prick bottom of dough with fork. Refrigerate 1 hour.

Preheat oven to 200°C/400°F/Gas Mark 6. Line tart shell with foil or parchment paper and fill with dry beans or rice. Bake 5 minutes, lift out foil with beans and bake 5 minutes longer, just until set. Remove to wire rack to cool slightly. Lower oven temperature to 190°C/375°F/Gas Mark 5.

In a bowl, beat together eggs, sugar, orange zest and orange-flavoured liqueur. Blend in the cream.

Sprinkle chopped chocolate evenly over bottom of tart shell, then sprinkle pine nuts over. Place tin on baking sheet and gently pour egg-and-cream mixture into shell.

Bake 30–35 minutes, until pastry is golden and egg mixture is set. Transfer to wire rack to cool 10 minutes.

Prepare decoration. With swivel-bladed vegetable peeler, remove thin strips of orange zest and cut into julienne strips. In a saucepan over high heat, bring strips, water and sugar to the boil. Boil 5–8 minutes, until syrup is thickened; stir in 15 ml/1 tbsp cold water.

With a pastry brush, glaze tart with sugar syrup and arrange julienne orange strips over top. Remove side of tin and slide tart onto plate. Serve tart warm.

CHOCOLATE AND PECAN PIE

8–10 SERVINGS

It hardly seems possible to improve on classic pecan pie, that is, of course, unless you add chocolate. The pastry is almost unsweetened to balance the rich filling. Serve with softly whipped cream.

150 g/5 oz plain flour
15 ml/1 tbsp caster sugar
2.5 ml/½ tsp salt
100 g/4 oz butter, cut into small pieces
120 ml/4 fl oz iced water

FILLING
75 g/3 oz plain chocolate, chopped
25 g/1 oz butter, cut into pieces
3 eggs
50 g/2 oz light brown sugar
75 ml/3 fl oz golden syrup
15 ml/1 tbsp vanilla essence
175 g/6 oz cups pecan halves
75 g/3 oz milk or plain chocolate chips
 (optional)

Prepare piecrust. In a food processor fitted with metal blade, process flour, sugar and salt to blend. Add butter and process 15–20 seconds, until mixture resembles coarse crumbs. With machine running, add iced water through feed tube, just until dough begins to stick together; *do not allow dough to form a ball* or pastry will be tough.

Turn dough onto floured work surface, shape into flat disc and wrap tightly in plastic wrap. Refrigerate 1 hour.

Lightly butter a 23 cm/9 in pie dish, 4 cm/1½ in deep. Soften dough 10–15 minutes at room temperature. On a well-floured surface, roll out dough into a 30 cm/12 in circle about 0.5 cm/¼ in thick. Roll dough loosely around rolling pin and unroll over pie dish; ease dough into dish.

With kitchen scissors, trim dough, leaving about a 0.5 cm/¼ in overhang; flatten to rim of pie dish pressing slightly toward centre of dish. With small knife, cut out hearts or other shapes from dough trimmings. Brush dough edge with water and press dough shapes to edge. Prick bottom of dough with fork. Refrigerate 30 minutes.

Preheat oven to 200°C/400°F/Gas Mark 6. Line pie shell with foil or parchment paper and fill with dry beans or rice. Bake 5 minutes, then lift out foil with beans and bake 5 minutes longer. Remove to wire rack to cool slightly. Lower oven temperature to 190°C/375°F/Gas Mark 5.

In a saucepan over low heat, melt chocolate and butter, stirring until smooth. Set aside.

In a bowl, beat together eggs, sugar, corn syrup and vanilla. Slowly beat in melted chocolate. Sprinkle pecan halves and chocolate chips (if using) over bottom of pastry. Place pie dish on baking sheet and carefully pour in chocolate mixture.

Bake 35–40 minutes, until chocolate mixture is set, top may crack slightly. If pastry edges begin to overbrown, cover with strips of foil. Transfer to wire rack to cool. Serve warm with softly whipped cream.

SWEET SUCCESS

For an extra rich treat, replace the plain pie crust with chocolate pie crust described on page 39.

CHOCOLATE CREAM PIE

8 SERVINGS

A classic, old-fashioned dessert; under a cloud of whipped cream is a deep, chocolate custard enclosed in a chocolate crumb crust. The whipped cream topping is lightened by adding beaten egg whites.

225 g/8 oz plain chocolate digestive biscuits
50 g/2 oz butter, melted
175 g/6 oz plain chocolate, chopped
250 ml/8 fl oz whipping cream
40 g/1½ oz cornflour
15 ml/1 tbsp plain flour
50 g/2 oz caster sugar
675 ml/22 fl oz milk
5 egg yolks
40 g/1½ oz butter, softened

LIGHT WHIPPED CREAM
350 ml/12 fl oz double cream
2 egg whites
1.5 ml/¼ tsp cream of tartar
50 g/2 oz sugar
10 ml/2 tsp vanilla essence
cocoa powder for dusting

Preheat oven to 180°C/350°F/Gas Mark 4. Lightly butter a 23 cm/9 in, 4 cm/1½ in deep pie dish or fluted baking dish.

In a food processor, process chocolate biscuits until fine crumbs form. Pour in melted butter and process just until blended. Pat onto bottom and sides of pie dish.

Bake 5–7 minutes, just until set. Transfer to wire rack to cool completely.

In a saucepan over low heat, melt chocolate with 250 ml/8 fl oz whipping cream, stirring until smooth. Set aside.

In another saucepan, combine cornflour, flour and sugar. Gradually stir in milk and cook over medium heat until thickened and bubbling.

In a bowl, beat egg yolks lightly. Slowly pour over 250 ml/8 fl oz hot milk into yolks, stirring constantly. Return egg-yolk mixture to pan and bring to a gentle boil, stirring constantly. Cook 1 minute longer. Stir in the butter and melted chocolate until well blended. Pour into prepared crust and place a piece of plastic wrap directly against

surface of filling to prevent a skin forming. Cool, then refrigerate until completely chilled.

With electric mixer, whip cream until soft peaks form. In another bowl with electric mixer and clean blades, beat egg whites and cream of tartar until stiff peaks form. Gradually sprinkle sugar over in 2 batches, beating well after each addition, until whites are stiff and glossy. Beat in vanilla.

Fold 1 spoonful of whites into cream to lighten, then fold remaining whites into cream. Peel plastic wrap from chilled custard; spread cream onto custard in a swirling pattern. Dust cream lightly with cocoa powder.

WHITE CHOCOLATE AND BANANA CREAM TART

8 SERVINGS

A luscious combination of a white chocolate-flavoured custard, bananas and whipped cream enclosed in a crisp pastry case with a little coconut for extra texture.

175 g/6 oz plain flour
65 g/2½ oz shredded sweetened
   coconut
100 g/4 oz butter, softened
30 ml/2 tbsp caster sugar
2 egg yolks
2.5 ml/½ tsp almond essence

WHITE CHOCOLATE CUSTARD
150 g/5 oz good quality white
   chocolate, chopped
120 ml/4 fl oz double cream
40 g/1½ oz cornflour
15 ml/1 tbsp plain flour
75 g/3 oz sugar
450 ml/16 fl oz milk
5 egg yolks
550 ml/20 fl oz whipping cream
2.5 ml/½ tsp almond essence
3 very ripe bananas
50 g/2 oz chopped almonds, toasted

Prepare pastry. With electric mixer at low speed, combine flour, coconut, butter, sugar, egg yolks and almond extract until well blended.

With fingers or back of a spoon, press dough onto bottom and side of a lightly-buttered, deep 23 cm/9 in, 4 cm/1½ in deep tart tin with removable bottom. Prick dough with fork. Refrigerate 30 minutes.

Preheat oven to 180°C/350°F/Gas Mark 4. Line tart shell with foil or parchment paper; fill with dry beans or rice. Bake 10 minutes. Carefully lift out foil with beans and bake 5–7 minutes longer, until golden. Remove to wire rack to cool completely.

Prepare custard. In a saucepan over low heat, melt white chocolate with cream, stirring until smooth. Set aside.

In another saucepan, combine cornflour, flour and sugar. Gradually stir in the milk and cook over medium heat until thickened and bubbling.

Beat egg yolks lightly. Slowly pour about 250 ml/8 fl oz hot milk into the yolks, stirring constantly. Return egg yolk mixture to the pan and bring to a gentle boil, stirring constantly. Cook 1–2 minutes longer. Stir in the melted chocolate until well blended. Cool to room temperature, stirring frequently to prevent a skin from forming.

With electric mixer, beat the whipping cream with the almond extract until soft peaks form. Fold about 120 ml/4 fl oz whipped cream into white chocolate custard.

Slice bananas and line bottom of pastry shell with the slices. Pour the white chocolate custard over and spread evenly. Remove side of tin and slide onto plate.

Spoon remaining cream into large piping bag fitted with a medium star tip. Pipe cream in scroll pattern in parallel rows, 1 cm/½ in apart. Sprinkle chopped toasted almonds between rows.

MOCHA-FUDGE PIE WITH ESPRESSO CUSTARD CREAM

10 SERVINGS

Even the most serious of chocolate lovers will be satisfied with this crustless, fudgy dessert. It is crisp on the outside but soft and brownie-like near the centre. The coffee custard cream is a welcome contrast to the rich, dense chocolate.

100 g/4 oz plain chocolate, chopped
100 g/4 oz butter, cut into pieces
4 eggs
15 ml/1 tbsp golden syrup
100 g/4 oz sugar
15 ml/1 tbsp instant espresso powder, dissolved in 15–30 ml/1–2 tbsp hot water
5 ml/1 tsp ground cinnamon
45 ml/3 tbsp milk

ESPRESSO CUSTARD CREAM
750 ml/1¼ pts milk
15 ml/1 tbsp instant espresso powder, dissolved in 15–30 ml/1–2 tbsp hot water
175 g/6 oz sugar
6 egg yolks
10 ml/2 tsp cornflour
30 ml/2 tbsp coffee-flavoured liqueur
whipped cream and chocolate coffee beans for garnish (optional)

Preheat oven to 180°C/350°F/Gas Mark 4. Lightly grease a 23 cm/9 in pie dish, 4 cm/1½ in deep.

In a saucepan over low heat, melt chocolate and butter, stirring until smooth. Set aside.

In a bowl, beat eggs lightly. Blend in corn syrup, sugar, dissolved espresso powder, cinnamon and milk. Stir in chocolate mixture until well blended. Place pie plate on a baking sheet. Pour chocolate mixture into pie plate.

Bake 20–25 minutes, or until the edge is set but centre is still almost liquid. Transfer to wire rack to cool completely; top may crack slightly.

Prepare custard. In a saucepan over medium heat, bring milk and dissolved espresso powder to the boil. In a bowl, beat sugar and egg yolks until pale and thick, 3–5 minutes. Stir in cornflour just until blended.

Slowly pour about 250 ml/8 fl oz hot milk into yolks, stirring constantly. Return yolk mixture to pan and cook over low heat, stirring constantly, until the sauce thickens, 5–8 minutes; *do not allow sauce to boil or it will curdle.* Strain into a *chilled* bowl and stir until slightly cool. Stir in coffee-flavoured liqueur and cool completely. Refrigerate until ready to serve.

To serve, place a spoonful of custard on a dessert plate and place a slice of tart on the pool of sauce. If you like, garnish with softly whipped cream and chocolate coffee beans.

SWEET SUCCESS

To help custard sauces to cool quickly and stop cooking instantly, strain the thickened custard into a metal bowl placed over another bowl of water with ice cubes; stir frequently until custard is just body temperature. This stops further cooking and prevents a skin from forming.

CHOCOLATE TRUFFLE TART

10 SERVINGS

A *pure chocolate truffle mixture is contained in a chocolate pastry in this delicious tart. The chocolate-on-chocolate drizzling is more for effect than flavour but the tart is equally delicious without it.*

100 g/4 oz plain flour
40 g/1½ oz cocoa powder
50 g/2 oz caster sugar
2.5 ml/½ tsp salt
100 g/4 oz well-chilled butter, cut into pieces
1 egg yolk
15–30 ml/1–2 tbsp iced water

TRUFFLE FILLING
300 ml/10 fl oz double cream
350 g/12 oz plain chocolate, chopped
40 g/1½ oz butter, cut into pieces
15–30 ml/1–2 tbsp orange-flavoured liqueur or brandy (optional)
25 g/1 oz good quality white chocolate, melted

Prepare pastry. Into a bowl, sift flour and cocoa powder. In a food processor fitted with metal blade, process flour mixture, sugar and salt to blend. Add butter and process 15–20 seconds, until mixture resembles coarse crumbs.

In another bowl, lightly beat egg yolk with 30 ml/2 tbsp iced water. Add to flour mixture and using *pulse action* process just until dough begins to stick together; *do not allow dough to form into a ball* or pastry will be tough. Dough should be soft and creamy and may be difficult to handle. Place a piece of plastic wrap on work surface. Turn out dough onto plastic wrap. Use plastic wrap to help shape dough into flat disc and wrap tightly. Refrigerate 1 to 2 hours.

Lightly grease a 23 cm/9 in tart tin, 4 cm/1½ in deep, with removable bottom. Soften dough 5–10 minutes at room temperature. Roll out dough between 2 sheets of waxed paper or plastic wrap to a 27.5 cm/11 in circle about 0.5 cm/¼ in thick. Peel off top sheet of waxed paper or plastic wrap and invert dough into pan. Remove bottom layer of paper or wrap. Press dough onto bottom and sides of tin. Prick bottom of dough with fork. Refrigerate 1 hour.

Preheat oven to 190°C/375°F/Gas Mark 5. Line tart shell with foil or parchment paper; fill with dried beans or rice. Bake 5–7 minutes; lift out foil with beans and bake 5–7 minutes longer, just until set; pastry may look slightly underdone on bottom, but it will dry out. Transfer to wire rack to cool completely.

In a saucepan over medium heat, bring cream to the boil. Remove pan from heat and stir in chocolate until melted and smooth. Stir in butter and liqueur.

Strain into tart shell; tilting slightly to even surface, but do not touch surface.

Spoon melted white chocolate into paper cone (see Decorating with Chocolate) and cut tip about 0.5 cm/¼ in in diameter. Drizzle white chocolate over surface of dark chocolate in an abstract design. Refrigerate 2–3 hours, until set. To serve, leave tart to soften slightly at room temperature, about 30 minutes.

SWEET SUCCESS

This tart can be made 2 days ahead and stored, covered, in the refrigerator. To store tarts or desserts without destroying the top or the decoration, place on a baking sheet and cover with a large overturned bowl.

WHITE CHOCOLATE MOUSSE AND STRAWBERRY TART

This is a luscious combination of white chocolate mousse and ripe, fragrant strawberries in a butter-rich crust. It can be made with other soft fruits such as raspberries or blackberries.

100 g/4 oz butter, softened
50 g/2 oz caster sugar
2.5 ml/½ tsp salt
3 egg yolks
5 ml/1 tsp vanilla essence
150 g/5 oz plain flour

WHITE CHOCOLATE MOUSSE FILLING
250 g/9 oz white chocolate, chopped
45 ml/3 tbsp cherry-flavoured liqueur
30 ml/2 tbsp water
350 ml/12 fl oz double cream
2 egg whites (optional)
1.5 ml/¼ tsp cream of tartar (optional)

STRAWBERRY FILLING
900 g/2 lbs fresh, ripe strawberries
30 ml/2 tbsp cherry-flavoured liqueur
25 g/1 oz white chocolate, melted, *or*
  White Chocolate Curls (see
  Decorating with Chocolate) *or*
  30 ml/2 tbsp seedless strawberry
  jam, melted and cooled, for
  decoration

Prepare pastry. In a bowl with a hand-held electric mixer, beat butter with sugar and salt until creamy, about 2 minutes. Add egg yolks and vanilla and beat until smooth. Add half the flour to the butter and egg mixture, then stir in remaining flour by hand until well blended.

Place a piece of plastic wrap on work surface. Scrape dough onto plastic wrap. Use plastic wrap to help shape dough into flat disc and wrap tightly. Refrigerate 1 hour.

Lightly butter a 25 cm/10 in tart tin with removable bottom. Soften dough 10 minutes at room temperature. On a well-floured surface, roll out dough to 28–30 cm/11½–12 in circle about 3 mm/⅛ in thick. Roll dough loosely around rolling pin and unroll over tart tin. Ease dough into tin, patching if necessary.

With floured fingers, press overhang down slightly toward centre, making top edge thicker. Roll rolling pin over tin edge to cut off excess dough. Press thicker top edge against side of tin to form rim about 0.5 cm/¼ in higher than tin. Using thumb and forefinger, crimp edge. Prick bottom of dough with fork. Refrigerate 1 hour.

Preheat oven to 190°C/375°F/Gas Mark 5. Line tart shell with foil or parchment paper; fill with dry beans or rice. Bake 10 minutes; lift out foil with beans and bake 5–7 minutes longer until set and golden. Remove to wire rack to cool completely.

Cut strawberries in half lengthwise. In a bowl, mash about 350 g/12 oz strawberry halves with 30 ml/2 tbsp cherry-flavoured liqueur. Set remaining berries and mashed berries aside.

Prepare mousse. In a saucepan over low heat, melt white chocolate with 45 ml/3 tbsp cherry-flavoured liqueur, water and 120 ml/4 fl oz cream, stirring until smooth. Set aside to cool.

With electric mixer, beat remaining cream until soft peaks form. Stir 1 spoonful of cream into the chocolate mixture to lighten, then fold in remaining cream. If you like, beat egg whites with the cream of tartar until stiff peaks form then fold them into the chocolate cream mixture to make a lighter, softer mousse.

Pour about one-third of the mousse mixture into the cooled tart shell. Spread mashed berries evenly over the mousse, then cover with the remaining mousse mixture.

To serve, arrange sliced strawberries cut side up in concentric circles around tart to cover mousse. Remove side of tin and slide tart onto serving plate. Spoon melted white chocolate into a paper cone (see Decorating with Chocolate) and drizzle white chocolate over tart; alternatively, decorate centre with white chocolate curls, or glaze with seedless strawberry preserves.

Be sure to allow the melted white chocolate to cool to below body temperature so it does not deflate the whipped cream. A small dab should feel cool when touched to your upper lip, about 30°C/85°F.
The tart shell can be made ahead, but the shell should be filled and assembled the same day to be served to prevent the berries from bleeding into the mousse mixture and the mousse from becoming too firm when refrigerated.

CHOCOLATE-CHOCOLATE CREAM PUFFS

With chocolate choux pastry and filled with a rich chocolate pastry cream, these cream puffs are then covered with a creamy chocolate topping. They can be made any size from mini to maxi!

100 g/4 oz plain flour
30 ml/2 tbsp cocoa powder
250 ml/8 fl oz water
2.5 ml/½ tsp salt
15 ml/1 tbsp sugar
100 g/4 oz butter, cut into pieces
5 eggs

CHOCOLATE PASTRY CREAM
150 g/5 oz plain chocolate, chopped
475 ml/16 fl oz milk
6 egg yolks
100 g/4 oz sugar
75 ml/5 tbsp plain flour
120 ml/4 fl oz whipping cream, whipped to soft peaks

CHOCOLATE SAUCE
50 g/2 oz butter, cut into pieces
225 g/8 oz plain chocolate, chopped
300 ml/10 fl oz whipping cream

Preheat oven to 220°C/425°F/Gas Mark 7. Lightly grease 2 large baking sheets.

Sift together flour and cocoa powder. In a saucepan over medium heat, bring water, salt, sugar and butter to the boil; the butter should just be melted when the water boils. Remove from heat and add flour mixture all at once, stirring vigorously until well blended and dough pulls away from side of pan. Return to the heat to cook 1 minute, stirring constantly. Remove from heat.

With an electric mixer or by hand, beat in eggs, 1 at a time, beating well after each addition; dough should be thick and shiny and just fall from a spoon.

Spoon dough into a large piping bag fitted with a star or plain tip. Pipe 12 mounds about 7.5 cm/3 in across, at least 5 cm/2 in apart onto baking sheets.

Bake 35–40 minutes, until puffed and firm. Turn off oven. Using a serrated knife, slice off top third of puff; return opened puffs, cut-sides up, onto baking sheet and return to oven 5–10 minutes to dry out. Transfer to wire rack to cool completely.

Prepare pastry cream. In the top of a double boiler over low heat, melt chocolate, stirring until smooth. Set aside. In a saucepan over medium heat, bring milk to the boil. In a bowl, beat egg yolks and sugar until pale and thick, 3–5 minutes. Stir in flour just until blended.

Slowly pour about 250 ml/8 fl oz hot milk into egg yolks, stirring constantly. Return yolk mixture to pan and cook over medium heat about 1 minute, until sauce thickens and boils, stirring constantly; remove from heat and quickly stir in melted chocolate until well blended. Strain into a large bowl and place a piece of plastic wrap directly against surface of cream to prevent a skin forming. Cool to room temperature. Carefully peel plastic wrap from cooled pastry cream. Fold in whipped cream.

Spoon cream into a large piping bag fitted with a large star or plain tip. Fill each puff bottom with pastry cream and cover each puff with its top. Arrange cream puffs on a large serving plate in a single layer or pile them on top of each other.

To serve, in a saucepan over low heat, melt chocolate and butter with cream until well blended. Remove from heat and cool 10–15 minutes, until slightly thickened. Pour sauce over cream puffs and serve while chocolate sauce is warm.

DOUBLE-CHOCOLATE BERRY TART WITH BLACKBERRY SAUCE

10–12 SERVINGS

This tart looks spectacular. It is worth searching for blackberries, boysenberries and loganberries when in season as they really do look and taste dramatic with the chocolate. Raspberries and blueberries can be used if other berries are unavailable.

100 g/4 oz butter, softened
100 g/4 oz caster sugar
2.5 ml/½ tsp salt
5 ml/1 tsp vanilla essence
75 g/3 oz cocoa powder
150 g/5 oz plain flour

CHOCOLATE GANACHE FILLING
550 ml/20 fl oz double cream
120 ml/4 fl oz seedless blackberry jam
225 g/8 oz bittersweet chocolate, chopped
25 g/1 oz butter, cut into pieces

BLACKBERRY SAUCE
225 g/8 oz fresh or frozen blackberries or raspberries
15 ml/1 tbsp lemon juice
30 ml/2 tbsp sugar
30 ml/2 tbsp blackberry or raspberry-flavoured liqueur
450 g/1 lb blackberries, loganberries and boysenberries, or any combination

Prepare pastry. In a food processor fitted with metal blade, process the butter, sugar, salt and vanilla until creamy. Add the cocoa powder and process 1 minute, until well blended; scrape side of bowl. Add flour all at once and using the *pulse action*, process 10–15 seconds, just until blended.

Place a piece of plastic wrap on work surface. Turn out dough onto plastic wrap. Use plastic wrap to help shape dough into flat disc and wrap tightly. Refrigerate 1 hour.

Lightly grease a 23 cm/9 in, 4 cm/1½ in deep tart tin with removable bottom. Soften dough 5–10 minutes, at room temperature. Roll out dough between 2 sheets of waxed paper or plastic wrap to a 27.5 cm/11 in circle about 0.5 cm/¼ in thick. Peel off top sheet of plastic wrap and invert dough into prepared tin. Ease dough into tin. Remove plastic wrap.

With floured fingers, press dough onto bottom and side of tin, then roll rolling pin over tin edge to cut off any excess dough. Prick bottom of dough with fork. Refrigerate 1 hour.

Preheat oven to 190°C/375°F/Gas Mark 5. Line tart shell with foil or parchment paper; fill with dry beans or rice. Bake 10 minutes; lift out foil with beans and bake 5 minutes longer, just until set. Pastry may look underdone on the bottom, it will dry out. Transfer to wire rack to cool completely.

Prepare filling. In a saucepan over medium heat, bring cream and black-berry jam to the boil. Remove from heat and add chocolate all at once, stirring until melted and smooth. Stir in butter, then strain into cooled tart, tilting tart to evenly distribute filling. Cool tart completely.

Prepare sauce. In a food processor, combine blackberries, lemon juice and sugar and process until smooth. Strain into a small bowl and add blackberry-flavoured liqueur. If sauce is too thick, thin with a little water.

To serve, arrange the berries on the top of the tart. With a pastry brush, brush berries with a little blackberry sauce to glaze lightly. Serve remaining sauce separately with tart.

BLACK-BOTTOM LEMON TARTLETS

The dark chocolate surprise beneath the creamy lemon custard is the black bottom in these flaky tartlet shells. Serve them on their own or more dramatically on a pool of chocolate-dotted lemon custard sauce.

175 g/6 oz plain flour
30 ml/2 tbsp icing sugar
2.5 ml/½ tsp salt
175 g/6 oz unsalted butter, cut into pieces and at room temperature
1 egg yolk
2.5 ml/½ tsp vanilla essence
30—45 ml/2—3 tbsp cold water

LEMON CUSTARD SAUCE
1 lemon
350 ml/12 fl oz milk
6 egg yolks
75 g/3 oz sugar

LEMON CURD FILLING
2 lemons
175 g/6 oz unsalted butter, cut into pieces
225 g/8 oz sugar
3 eggs

CHOCOLATE FILLING
175 ml/6 fl oz cream
175 g/6 oz plain chocolate, chopped
25 g/1 oz unsalted butter, cut into pieces
Chocolate Triangles (see Decorating with Chocolate) for decoration
25 g/1 oz plain chocolate, melted

SWEET SUCCESS

Pastry and tartlets can be prepared a day ahead. These tartlets are best filled just a few hours before serving so fillings are still soft.
An easy way to blind bake tartlets is to use cup cake paper cases. One small paper case just covers the bottom and sides of a 7.5 cm/3 in tartlet mould.

Prepare custard sauce. With a swivel-bladed vegetable peeler, remove strips of zest from lemon. Place in a medium saucepan over medium heat with the milk and bring to the boil. Remove from heat and leave 5 minutes to infuse. Re-heat milk gently.

With an electric mixer, beat egg yolks and sugar until pale and thick, 2–3 minutes. Pour about 250 ml/8 fl oz hot milk over, beating vigorously. Return egg yolk mixture to pan and cook gently over low heat, stirring constantly with a wooden spoon until mixture thickens and lightly coats the back of the spoon; do not let it boil or it will curdle. Strain into a chilled bowl. Squeeze 30 ml/2 tbsp juice from the lemon and stir into sauce. Cool; stirring occasionally. Refrigerate until ready to use.

Prepare lemon curd filling. Grate the zest and squeeze the juice of the lemons into the top of a double boiler. Add butter and sugar and stir over medium heat until the butter is melted and sugar dissolved. Lower heat. In a bowl, lightly beat the eggs, then strain into butter mixture. Cook over low heat, stirring constantly with a wooden spoon until mixture thickens and coats the back of the spoon, about 15 minutes. Pour (or strain if you do not want the lemon zest) into a bowl. Cool, stirring occasionally. Refrigerate to thicken.

Prepare pastry. Place flour, sugar and salt into a food processor fitted with metal blade. Process to blend. Add butter and process 15–20 seconds, until mixture resembles coarse crumbs. In a bowl, beat the yolk with the vanilla and water. With machine running, pour yolk mixture through feed tube just until dough begins to stick together; *do not allow dough to form a ball* or pastry will be tough. If dough appears too dry add 15–30 ml/1–2 tbsp more cold water, little by little, just until dough holds together.

Place a piece of plastic wrap on a work surface. Turn dough out onto plastic wrap. Use plastic wrap to help shape dough into a flat disc. Wrap tightly and refrigerate at least 30 minutes.

Lightly butter twelve 7.5 cm/3 in tartlet tins (if possible, with removable bottoms). On a lightly floured surface, roll out pastry to an oblong shape slightly more than 3 mm/⅛ in thick. Using a 10 cm/4 in fluted cutter, cut out 12 circles and press each one onto bottom and sides of tartlet tins. Prick bottom of dough with a fork. Place tins on a large baking sheet and refrigerate 30 minutes.

Preheat oven to 190°C/375°F/Gas Mark 5. Cut out twelve 12.5 cm/5 in circles of foil and line each tin; fill with dry beans or rice. Bake 5–8 minutes; remove foil with beans and bake 5 minutes longer, until golden. Transfer tartlets to wire rack to cool.

Prepare chocolate filling. In a saucepan over medium heat, bring cream to the boil. Remove from heat and stir in chocolate all at once until melted and smooth. Beat in butter and leave to cool slightly.

Spoon an equal amount of chocolate filling into each tartlet to cover bottom and make a layer about 0.5 cm/¼ in thick. Refrigerate 10 minutes to allow chocolate layer to set.

Onto each chocolate-filled tartlet, spoon over a layer of lemon curd to come just to the top of the pastry. Set aside, but do not refrigerate or chocolate layer will be too firm.

Spoon a little custard onto dessert plate. Remove tartlet from tin and place in centre of plate. Decorate each tartlet with a chocolate triangle. If you like, spoon melted chocolate into a paper cone (see Decorating with Chocolate), cut 3 mm/⅛ in opening and make drops of chocolate in a circle 2.5 cm/1 in from the edge of plate. Draw a cocktail stick or skewer through chocolate to marble into the custard or make "heart" motif.

Desserts

HOT CHOCOLATE SOUFFLE WITH WHITE CHOCOLATE AND ORANGE SAUCE

CHOCOLATE CRÊPES WITH PINEAPPLE AND BITTER CHOCOLATE SAUCE

TRUFFLE-FILLED POACHED PEARS

CHOCOLATE PAVLOVA WITH KIWI FRUIT AND ORANGE

APRICOT-GLAZED WHITE CHOCOLATE RICE PUDDING WITH BITTER CHOCOLATE SAUCE

CHOCOLATE TIRAMISÙ

TRIPLE CHOCOLATE MOUSSE PARFAITS

WHITE CHOCOLATE FRUIT FOOLS IN CHOCOLATE CUPS

CHOCOLATE AND RASPBERRY CHARLOTTE

PEACHES 'N' WHITE CHOCOLATE CREAM MERINGUES

VELVETY CHOCOLATE MOUSSE

CHOCOLATE BOX WITH WHITE CHOCOLATE MOUSSE AND BERRIES

FRUIT-STUDDED CHOCOLATE MARQUISE WITH BOURBON CUSTARD CREAM

FRUITED WHITE CHOCOLATE BAVARIAN CREAMS WITH PASSION FRUIT AND CHOCOLATE SAUCES

CHOCOLATE POTS DE CRÈME

CHOCOLATE-GLAZED CHOCOLATE ZUCCOTTO

HOT CHOCOLATE SOUFFLÉ WITH WHITE CHOCOLATE AND ORANGE SAUCE

6 SERVINGS

This elegant dessert is surprisingly simple to make, and, although it must be served immediately when baked, it can be prepared several hours ahead, leaving only the egg whites to be beaten and folded in at the last moment. The extra chocolate sauce is optional.

granulated sugar for sprinkling dish
100 g/4 oz plain chocolate, chopped
50 g/2 oz unsalted butter, cut into
    pieces
4 eggs, separated
30 ml/2 tbsp orange-flavoured liqueur
1.5 ml/¼ tsp cream of tartar
30 ml/2 tbsp sugar
icing sugar for dusting

CHOCOLATE AND ORANGE SAUCE
75 g/3 oz good quality white chocolate,
    chopped
75 ml/2½ fl oz whipping cream
30 ml/2 tbsp orange-flavoured liqueur
30 ml/2 tbsp orange juice

Preheat oven to 240°C/475°F/Gas Mark 9. Generously butter bottom and sides of a 1 l/1¾ pt soufflé dish. Refrigerate 5 minutes to set butter, then re-butter dish. Lightly sprinkle bottom and sides of dish with sugar, then shake out any excess.

In a saucepan over low heat, melt the chocolate and butter, stirring frequently until smooth. Remove from heat. Beat in egg yolks and orange-flavoured liqueur. Set aside to cool slightly, stirring occasionally.

With electric mixer, beat egg whites and cream of tartar together until stiff peaks form. Sprinkle sugar over and continue beating 1 minute, until sugar is incorporated and whites are glossy.

Fold one-quarter of beaten whites into cooled chocolate mixture to lighten, then fold in remaining whites. Do not overwork mixture; it is better to have a few streaks of white than to deflate the mixture. Pour into the prepared dish.

Place on a baking sheet and bake 5 minutes. Reduce temperature to 220°C/425°F/Gas Mark 7 and bake 10–12 minutes longer. Top of soufflé should be set but the soufflé should jiggle when baking sheet is moved; it should remain soft in the centre.

Meanwhile, prepare sauce. In a saucepan over low heat, melt chocolate with cream, stirring frequently until smooth. Stir in orange-flavoured liqueur and juice. Strain into a sauceboat and set aside to keep warm.

To serve, fold a dinner napkin or doilly on a serving plate to prevent soufflé from sliding on plate. Dust top of soufflé with icing sugar. Transfer from baking sheet to prepared serving plate. Serve soufflé immediately; pass sauce separately.

SWEET SUCCESS

To serve a soufflé "French-style," use a serving spoon to "crack" the top, much like cracking a soft-boiled egg. Serve some of the firmer outside and the softer centre to each guest and pass any sauce separately.

Soufflés make a spectacular presentation when served in individual dishes. Prepare six 150 ml/5 fl oz ramekins as directed, but bake 10–12 minutes at 220°C/425°F/Gas Mark 7.

CHOCOLATE CRÊPES WITH PINEAPPLE AND BITTER CHOCOLATE SAUCE

MAKES 12 CREPES

The combination of chocolate and pineapple is delicious. The addition of chocolate chips and toasted macadamias adds texture and flavour when the crêpes are heated. Serve with the hot chocolate sauce.

105 ml/7 tbsp plain flour
15 ml/1 tbsp cocoa powder
5 ml/1 tsp sugar
1.5 ml/¼ tsp salt
2 eggs
175 ml/6 fl oz milk
25 g/1 oz unsalted butter, melted, plus
    extra for reheating crêpes
5 ml/1 tsp vanilla essence
vegetable oil for greasing pan

PINEAPPLE FILLING
1 pineapple, peeled, cored and cut into
    1 cm/½ in pieces or 450 g/1 lb can
    pineapple pieces in juice, drained
25 g/1 oz unsalted butter
2.5 ml/½ tsp ground cinnamon
60 ml/2 fl oz natural maple syrup
50 g/2 oz plain or milk chocolate chips
50 g/2 oz macadamia nuts, chopped
    and toasted

CHOCOLATE SAUCE
100 g/4 oz plain chocolate, chopped
75 ml/2½ fl oz water
30 ml/2 tbsp natural maple syrup
25 g/1 oz unsalted butter, cut into
    pieces
icing sugar for dusting
fresh cranberries or raspberries and
    mint leaves for decoration

Into a bowl, sift flour, cocoa powder, sugar and salt. Mix to blend; make a well in centre.

In another bowl, lightly beat the eggs with the milk. Gradually add to the well in the centre of flour mixture. Using a whisk, blend in flour from sides of bowl to form a paste, then a batter; beat until smooth. Stir in melted butter and vanilla and strain into another bowl. Leave to stand 1 hour.

With a pastry brush, brush the bottom of a 17.5 or 20 cm/7 or 8 in crêpe pan with a little vegetable oil. Heat pan over medium heat. Stir batter (if batter is too thick, stir in a little milk or water; it should be thin). Fill a 60 ml/2 fl oz measure or small ladle three-quarters full with batter, then pour into hot pan. Quickly tilt and rotate pan to cover bottom of pan with a thin layer of batter. Cook over medium-high heat 1–2 minutes, until top is set and bottom is golden. With a palette knife, loosen edge of crêpe from pan, turn over and cook 30–45 seconds, just until set. Turn out onto plate.

Continue making crêpes, stirring batter occasionally and brushing pan lightly with oil. (A non-stick pan is ideal and does not need additional greasing.) Stack crêpes with sheets of waxed paper between each. Set aside.

Prepare filling. In a large frying pan over medium-high heat, melt butter until sizzling. Add pineapple pieces and sauté until golden, 3–4 minutes.

Sprinkle with cinnamon and stir in maple syrup. Cook 1–2 minutes longer, until pineapple is lightly coated with syrup and liquid has evaporated. Remove from heat.

Lay a crêpe on a plate or work surface, bottom side down. Spoon a little pineapple mixture onto top half of crêpe. Sprinkle over a few chocolate chips and macadamia nuts. Fold bottom half over, then fold into quarters. Continue using all the crêpes, pineapple filling, chocolate chips and nuts. Set each one on a buttered baking sheet and cover tightly with foil until ready to serve.

Prepare chocolate sauce. In a medium saucepan over low heat, melt chocolate with water and maple syrup, stirring frequently until smooth and well blended. Stir in butter. Keep warm.

Preheat oven to 190°C/375°F/Gas Mark 5. Uncover crêpes, brush top of each with melted butter and re-cover tightly. Bake 5 minutes just until heated through. Place on a dessert plate or individual plates. Dust with icing sugar and decorate with fresh cranberries or raspberries and mint leaves. Serve chocolate sauce separately.

TRUFFLE-FILLED POACHED PEARS

6 SERVINGS

These richly coloured port-poached pears are filled with a luscious chocolate-truffle surprise. For a really full flavour, the pears should be poached a day ahead and left to soak up the port syrup overnight.

thinly pared strips of zest and juice of 1
   lemon
thinly pared strips of zest and juice of 1
   orange
1 cinnamon stick
4–5 whole cloves
½ bottle tawny port wine
100 g/4 oz sugar
120 ml/4 fl oz redcurrant jelly or
   seedless raspberry jam
475–750 ml/16–24 fl oz water
6 firm pears, all the same size

CHOCOLATE TRUFFLE FILLING
45 ml/3 tbsp whipping cream
60 ml/2 fl oz reserved poaching syrup
175 g/6 oz plain chocolate, chopped
25 g/1 oz unsalted butter, cut into
   pieces
Chocolate Leaves (see Decorating with
   Chocolate) for decoration

In a saucepan large enough to hold pears in a single layer, combine lemon and orange zests and juices, cinnamon stick, cloves, port wine, sugar, redcurrant jelly and water; there should be enough liquid to cover pears. Bring to the boil, boil 1–2 minutes, then lower heat to a simmer.

Slice bottom from each pear so it stands flat. With a swivel-bladed vegetable peeler, peel pears and core from bottom end leaving stem attached. Drop pears into poaching syrup and cover with a circle of waxed paper with a slit made in the centre (this keeps pears under the liquid). Bring pears to the boil, then reduce heat to low and simmer 15–20 minutes, just until tender or when sharp knife enters flesh easily. Remove from heat and cool pears in poaching liquid, 3–4 hours.

Transfer pears from liquid to a large bowl. Bring syrup to the boil and reduce 20 minutes over high heat, until syrup is thickened and coats the back of a spoon lightly. Strain over pears and leave to cool to room temperature. Refrigerate overnight.

Prepare chocolate filling. In a saucepan over medium heat, bring cream and poaching syrup to the boil. Add chocolate, stirring until melted and smooth. Beat in butter. Refrigerate 1 hour, until chocolate is thick enough to pipe.

Remove pears from their liquid to wire rack placed over a baking sheet to catch any drips. Spoon chocolate into medium piping bag fitted with medium plain nozzle and gently pipe chocolate mixture into centre of pears. Reserve any left over chocolate. Stand each pear on a plate.

To serve, pour a little poaching syrup onto one side of each plate. Gently reheat any left over chocolate-truffle mixture and spoon a little over each pear. Garnish each pear with a chocolate leaf near stem. Place other leaves on plate if you like.

SWEET SUCCESS

It is best to poach pears 1 day ahead or at least early on the day of serving so the pears have a chance to cool and absorb the poaching liquid. They should have an almost translucent quality and the syrup should be thickened to a glazing consistency.

CHOCOLATE PAVLOVA WITH KIWI FRUIT AND ORANGE

8 TO 10 SERVINGS

Both Australia and New Zealand claim to have invented this delicate meringue-based dessert, named for the ballerina Anna Pavlova. I have added cocoa powder to the meringue, filled it with chocolate cream and topped it with a mixture of fruits, tiny wallflowers and herbs.

45 ml/3 tbsp cocoa powder
5 ml/1 tsp cornflour
4 egg whites, at room temperature
1.5 ml/¼ tsp salt
225 g/8 oz caster sugar
5 ml/1 tsp cider vinegar

WHITE CHOCOLATE CREAM
100 g/4 oz fine-quality white chocolate, chopped
120 ml/4 fl oz milk
15 g/½ oz unsalted butter, cut into pieces
50 g/2 oz icing sugar, sifted
250 ml/8 fl oz double cream
2 kiwi fruit, peeled and sliced
2 oranges, segmented
fresh mint sprigs for decoration
wallflowers

Preheat oven to 170°C/325°F/Gas Mark 3. Place a sheet of non-stick parchment paper on a large baking sheet and mark a 20 cm/8 in circle on it using a plate or cake tin as a guide. Into a bowl, sift together cocoa powder and cornflour; set aside.

In another bowl with electric mixer, beat egg whites until frothy. Add salt and continue beating until stiff peaks form. Sprinkle in sugar, 15 ml/1 tbsp at a time, making sure each addition is well blended before adding the next, until stiff and glossy. Fold in cocoa and cornflour mixture, then fold in vinegar.

Spoon mixture onto the circle on the paper, spreading the meringue evenly and building up the sides higher than the centre. Bake in centre of oven 45–50 minutes, until set. Turn off the oven and leave meringue to stand in the oven 45 minutes longer; the meringue may crack or sink.

Meanwhile, prepare chocolate cream. In a saucepan over low heat, melt chocolate with milk, stirring until smooth. Beat in butter and cool completely.

Remove meringue from oven. Using a palette knife, transfer to a serving plate. Cut a circle around centre of meringue about 5 cm/2 in from edge; this allows the centre to sink gently without pulling the edges in.

When the chocolate mixture is completely cool, in a bowl with electric mixer, beat cream until soft peaks form. Stir half the cream into the chocolate to lighten, then fold in remaining cream. Spoon into centre of meringue.

Arrange kiwi fruit and orange in centre over the chocolate cream and decorate with fresh mint and wallflowers.

SWEET SUCCESS

For a more elegant presentation, pipe meringue into a 23 cm/9 in round using a large star tip.

APRICOT-GLAZED WHITE CHOCOLATE RICE PUDDING WITH BITTER CHOCOLATE SAUCE

10 SERVINGS

The addition of white chocolate to rice pudding transforms a homely dessert into an elegant one. The apricot glaze and chocolate sauce are the perfect foil to the sweet, creamy pudding. Soak the raisins overnight for the fullest flavour.

100 g/4 oz sultanas

45 ml/3 tbsp hot water

30 ml/2 tbsp apricot brandy or
    orange-flavoured liqueur

150 g/5 oz medium- or long-grain white
    rice

350 ml/12 fl oz milk

250 ml/8 fl oz water

25 g/1 oz butter

100 g/4 oz sugar

175 g/6 oz good-quality white
    chocolate, chopped

3 eggs

475 ml/16 fl oz double cream

10 ml/2 tsp vanilla essence

5 ml/1 tsp ground cinnamon

2.5 ml/½ tsp grated nutmeg

APRICOT GLAZE

120 ml/4 fl oz apricot jam

15 ml/1 tbsp orange juice or water

15 ml/1 tbsp apricot brandy or orange-
    flavoured liqueur

BITTER CHOCOLATE SAUCE

175 ml/6 fl oz double cream

175 ml/6 fl oz apricot jam

175 g/6 oz bittersweet chocolate,
    chopped

30 ml/2 tbsp apricot brandy or orange-
    flavoured liqueur

In a bowl, combine sultanas, hot water and apricot brandy. Leave to stand at least 2 hours.

In a heavy bottomed saucepan, combine rice, 250 ml/8 fl oz milk, water, butter and 50 g/2 oz sugar. Bring to the boil, stirring occasionally. Reduce heat, cover and simmer 18–20 minutes, just until liquid is absorbed.

Meanwhile, preheat oven to 150°C/300°F/Gas Mark 2. Butter a 1.5–2 l/2½–3½ pt shallow baking dish or soufflé dish and set aside. In a saucepan over low heat, melt chocolate with remaining milk, stirring frequently until smooth. Remove from heat. In a large bowl, lightly beat eggs, remaining sugar, cream, vanilla, cinnamon and nutmeg. Slowly beat in melted chocolate until well blended. Stir in the sultanas and any liquid. Stir egg mixture into cooked rice mixture until well blended, then pour into baking dish. Cover with foil.

Set baking dish into a roasting tin. Fill tin with hot water to about halfway up the side of the dish. Bake 30 minutes, uncover and bake 15–20 minutes longer, until a knife inserted 5 cm/2 in from the edge of dish comes out clean; centre should remain slightly moist. Run sharp knife around edge of dish to loosen pudding from edge and prevent centre from splitting. Leave to cool 1 hour.

Meanwhile, prepare glaze. In a saucepan over medium heat, melt apricot jam with orange juice and apricot brandy, stirring until smooth. Gently spoon over top of pudding to glaze.

Prepare chocolate sauce. In a saucepan over low heat, bring cream and apricot jam to a boil. Remove from the heat and stir in chocolate, stirring until melted and smooth. Press through a sieve and stir in apricot brandy; keep warm. Serve with glazed rice pudding.

SWEET SUCCESS

This pudding can be made in individual moulds and unmoulded for a more elegant presentation. Butter ten 150 ml/5 fl oz custard cups or ramekins and line bottom of each with waxed or parchment paper. Butter paper. Bake 3–5 minutes less than for above recipe. Cool puddings at least 1 hour; do not glaze. Unmould each pudding onto a plate, remove paper and top with a little warm glaze; spread evenly. Pour over a little chocolate sauce and serve remainder separately.

CHOCOLATE TIRAMISÙ

A classic Italian dessert which has become so popular everywhere there must be hundreds of variations. This one combines chocolate with the traditional coffee flavour and does not use any uncooked eggs in the creamy filling so it can be prepared days ahead. It should be soft but firm enough to slice and hold its shape.

CHOCOLATE SPONGE FINGERS

75 g/3½ oz plain flour
25 g/1 oz cocoa powder
15 ml/1 tbsp instant espresso or coffee powder
1.5 ml/¼ tsp salt
4 eggs, separated
100 g/4 oz caster sugar
10 ml/2 tsp vanilla essence
1.5 ml/¼ tsp cream of tartar
icing sugar for dusting

CHOCOLATE MASCARPONE FILLING

490 g/17½ oz container mascarpone cheese, at room temperature
75 g/3 oz icing sugar, sifted
350 ml/12 fl oz freshly brewed expresso or instant coffee
550 ml/20 fl oz double cream
175 g/6 oz plain chocolate, melted and cooled
90 ml/6 tbsp coffee-flavoured liqueur
50 g/2 oz plain chocolate, grated
30 ml/2 tbsp chocolate-flavoured liqueur
cocoa powder for dusting
whipped cream for decoration (optional)

Prepare spongefingers. Grease 2 large baking sheets. Line with waxed or parchment paper. Grease and lightly flour paper. In a bowl, sift together *twice* flour, cocoa powder, espresso powder and salt. Mix well and set aside.

In another bowl with electric mixer, beat egg yolks with 50 g/2 oz sugar until thick and pale, 2–3 minutes. Beat in vanilla.

In a large bowl with electric mixer and cleaned beaters, beat egg whites and cream of tartar until stiff peaks form. Sprinkle over remaining sugar, 30 ml/2 tbsp at a time, beating well after each addition.

Fold 1 spoonful egg whites into egg-yolk mixture to lighten, then fold in remaining whites. Sift flour mixture over and fold into yolk-white mixture, but do not overwork mixture. Spoon batter into a large piping bag fitted with a medium (about 1 cm/½ in) plain nozzle. Pipe batter into about thirty 12.5 cm/ 5 in or twenty-four 10 cm/4 in sponge fingers. Dust with icing sugar.

Bake 12–15 minutes, until set and tops feel firm when touched with a fingertip. Transfer to wire rack to cool on baking sheets 10 minutes. With a wide spatula, transfer sponge fingers to wire racks to cool completely.

With hand-held electric mixer at low speed, beat mascarpone cheese with icing sugar just until smooth. Gradually beat in 60 ml/2 fl oz espresso or coffee powder; do not overbeat.

In another bowl with electric mixer, beat cream until soft peaks form. Gently fold cream into mascarpone mixture. Divide mixture in half. Fold melted chocolate and 30 ml/2 tbsp coffee-flavour liqueur into half until blended. Fold grated chocolate and chocolate-flavoured liqueur into remaining mascarpone mixture. Set both mixtures aside.

Into a bowl or pie dish wide enough to hold the sponge fingers, combine *half*

the remaining espresso coffee with 30 ml/2 tbsp coffee-flavoured liqueur. Quickly dip one side of a sponge finger into coffee mixture and place it dry-side down in a 32.5 × 23 cm/13 × 9 in baking dish; do not let sponge fingers get too soggy or they may fall apart. Continue with about half the sponge fingers (you will need enough for 2 layers) to form a fairly close layer with not much space between each sponge finger. Drizzle over remaining espresso mixture. Place remaining espresso- and 30 ml/ 2 tbsp coffee-flavoured liqueur into pie dish.

Pour chocolate-mascarpone mixture over the bottom layer of sponge fingers smoothing the chocolate mixture. Layer remaining sponge fingers over the chocolate layers, dipping each one into the espresso mixture 1 at a time. Drizzle over any remaining expresso mixture. Pour remaining grated chocolate-mascarpone mixture over this layer and smooth the top leaving no spaces between filling and sides of dish. Cover dish tightly and refrigerate overnight. Dust top with cocoa powder before serving. If you like, decorate with extra whipped cream.

Mascarpone is an Italian cream cheese with a smooth creamy texture and soft, sweet flavour. It is available from supermarkets and speciality stores. A quicker version can be made using about 200 g/7 oz bought sponge fingers. In either case, make this dessert at least 1 day ahead to allow the mixture to set firm and the flavours to mingle.

TRIPLE CHOCOLATE MOUSSE PARFAITS

6 SERVINGS

This trio of delicate chocolate mousses is served in sundae, parfait or wine glasses to show off the layers. It could be equally impressive layered in a larger straight-sided glass bowl — either way, it is worth the effort.

BITTERSWEET CHOCOLATE MOUSSE
100 g/4 oz bittersweet chocolate, chopped
60 ml/2 fl oz whipping cream
15 g/½ oz unsalted butter, cut into pieces
2 eggs, separated
15 ml/1 tbsp rum
pinch cream of tartar

MILK CHOCOLATE MOUSSE
100 g/4 oz good quality milk chocolate, chopped
60 ml/2 fl oz whipping cream
25 g/1 oz unsalted butter, cut into pieces
2 eggs, separated
15 ml/1 tbsp coffee-flavoured liqueur
pinch cream of tartar

WHITE CHOCOLATE MOUSSE
100 g/4 oz good quality white chocolate, chopped
60 ml/2 fl oz whipping cream
15 ml/1 tbsp unsalted butter, cut into pieces
2 eggs, separated
15 ml/1 tbsp chocolate-flavoured liqueur
pinch of cream of tartar
90 ml/6 tbsp chocolate sauce
60 ml/2 fl oz whipped cream
6 chocolate coffee beans

Prepare bittersweet chocolate mousse. In a saucepan, melt chocolate with cream, stirring frequently until smooth. Remove from heat. Stir in butter and beat in egg yolks, 1 at a time, then stir in rum. Allow to cool.

With electric mixer, beat whites and cream of tartar until stiff peaks form; do not overbeat. Stir in 1 spoonful of whites into the chocolate mixture to lighten, then fold in remaining whites.

Using a ladle or tablespoon, carefully spoon an equal amount of mousse into each of 6 sundae, parfait or wine glasses. Do not touch edge of glass; if any of the mixture drips, wipe glass clean. Place glasses on a tray or baking sheet and refrigerate 1 hour, or until firmly set.

Prepare milk chocolate mousse as above, then spoon equal amounts over bittersweet chocolate mousse. Refrigerate about 1 hour, until set.

Prepare white chocolate mousse as above, then spoon equal amounts over the milk chocolate mousse. Cover each glass with plastic wrap and refrigerate 4–6 hours or overnight, until set.

To serve, spoon 15 ml/1 tbsp chocolate sauce over each mousse. Spoon whipped cream into a small piping bag fitted with a medium star nozzle and pipe a rosette of cream onto each mousse. Garnish with chocolate coffee beans.

WHITE CHOCOLATE FRUIT FOOLS IN CHOCOLATE CUPS

12 SERVINGS

Fruit fools are a dessert made from a fruit purée folded into whipped cream. This elegant version combines white chocolate mousse and three fruit purées presented in chocolate cups. Use any fruit combination you like.

12 Chocolate Cups (see Decorating with Chocolate)

MANGO PURÉE

1 mango, peeled and cut into cubes, with 4 cubes reserved for garnish
grated zest and juice of ½ orange
5 ml/1 tsp lemon juice or to taste
15 ml/1 tbsp sugar or to taste

KIWI FRUIT PURÉE

3 kiwi fruit, peeled and sliced with 4 slices reserved for decoration
grated zest of 1 lime with 5—10 ml/ 1—2 tsp juice
15 ml/1 tbsp sugar or to taste

CRANBERRY-RASPBERRY PURÉE

100 g/4 oz fresh raspberries with berries reserved for garnish
15 ml/1 tbsp lemon juice
5 ml/1 tsp sugar or to taste
225 g/8 oz can cranberry sauce

WHITE CHOCOLATE MOUSSE

100 g/4 oz good quality white chocolate, chopped
60 ml/2 fl oz milk
15 ml/1 tbsp orange-flavoured liqueur
300 ml/10 fl oz double cream
2 egg whites
1.5 ml/¼ tsp cream of tartar

Prepare chocolate cups as directed on page 11, using 675 g/1½ lbs plain chocolate and 30 ml/1 tbsp white vegetable fat and extra large muffin-tin paper cases.

Prepare fruit purées in a food processor or blender, beginning with the lightest colour purée to avoid washing the processor after each purée. Place mango cubes in the processor with orange zest and juice. Process until smooth. Taste purée and add lemon juice and sugar if necessary; this depends on the natural sweetness of the fruit. Scrape purée into a bowl. Cover and refrigerate.

Place kiwi fruit slices into the processor with lime zest and juice. Process until smooth. Taste purée and add more lime juice and sugar if necessary. Scrape purée into a bowl. Cover and refrigerate.

Place the raspberries, lemon juice and sugar into the food processor. Process until smooth. Press through a strainer into a bowl. Return to food processor. Add the cranberry sauce and using the *pulse action*, process once or twice, just to blend, but leaving some texture to the purée. Taste purée and add more lemon juice or sugar if necessary. Scrape purée into small bowl. Cover and refrigerate.

Prepare mousse. In a saucepan over low heat, melt white chocolate with milk, stirring frequently until smooth. Remove from heat and stir in orange-flavoured liqueur. Cool to room temperature.

With hand-held electric mixer, beat cream until soft peaks form. Stir 1 spoonful of cream into chocolate mixture to lighten, then fold in remaining cream.

In another bowl with electric mixer with clean beaters, beat egg whites and cream of tartar until stiff peaks form. Fold into chocolate-cream mixture. (You may not want to use *all* the egg whites if the mousse is soft enough; this depends on the brand of chocolate used.) Divide into 3 bowls.

To assemble, arrange the prepared chocolate cups on 1 large or 2 smaller baking sheets (arrange adequate refrigerator space beforehand). Spoon a little of the mango purée into 4 chocolate cups. Spoon a little of the raspberry into 4 of the chocolate cups and then the kiwi fruit purée into the remaining 4 cups. Reserve a little of each purée for topping, then fold each of the purées into one of each of the 3 bowls of mousse; *do not mix well*, leave swirls of purée visible for effect. Spoon each fool mixture into the appropriate chocolate cups and top each with a decorative swirl of its matching purée. Refrigerate until ready to serve. Decorate each with a berry, cube or slice of fruit. Refrigerate at least 30 minutes or until firm.

SWEET SUCCESS

Pretty chocolate cups can be made using brioche moulds or teacups. Line each mould or cup with a square of foil. Do not press tightly but allow it to form folds or soft pleats against the side of the mould or cup; be sure the bottom is flat. Spoon melted chocolate down the inside of the folds using a zig-zag motion and turning the cup. This gives an uneven pleated look.

WHITE CHOCOLATE FRUIT FOOLS IN CHOCOLATE CUPS ▶

CHOCOLATE AND RASPBERRY CHARLOTTE

8–10 SERVINGS

This creamy chocolate-raspberry charlotte is easy to make, but stunning enough for a very special occasion. Tie a satin ribbon around the sponge fingers before serving for an unusual presentation.

vegetable oil for tin
200 g/7 oz sponge fingers
225 g/8 oz package frozen raspberries,
    sprinkled with 30 ml/2 tbsp sugar
    then defrosted
120 ml/4 fl oz seedless raspberry jam
350 g/12 oz plain chocolate, chopped
60 ml/2 fl oz raspberry-flavoured
    liqueur
60 ml/2 fl oz water
2 eggs, separated, plus 2 whites
1.5 ml/¼ tsp cream of tartar
120 ml/4 fl oz double cream
120 ml/4 fl oz double cream, whipped,
    for decoration
225 g/8 oz fresh raspberries for
    decoration

Lightly oil sides of a 20 cm/8 in spring-form tin. Gently separate the sponge fingers lengthwise, but do not separate them if they are joined side-by-side. Trim bottom of the sponge fingers so they sit flat against the bottom of tin.

Line the sides of the tin with sponge fingers, fitting tightly so no spaces exist. Line bottom of tin with remaining sponge fingers, cutting them to fit if necessary. Be sure there are not any spaces.

Drain frozen raspberries in a strainer. Into a saucepan, bring raspberry syrup and raspberry jam to the boil. Boil 2–3 minutes, until sauce is thickened and syrupy. Remove from heat and cool slightly. With a pastry brush, brush sponge fingers on bottom of tin with syrup. Set aside.

In a saucepan over low heat, melt chocolate with raspberry-flavoured liqueur and water, stirring frequently until smooth. Set aside. In a bowl, beat egg yolks 2–3 minutes, until pale and thick. Slowly beat in melted chocolate until well blended. Set aside.

In another bowl with hand-held electric mixer, beat cream until soft peaks form. Stir 1 spoonful of cream into chocolate mixture to lighten. Set remaining cream aside.

In another bowl with electric mixer, beat egg whites and cream of tartar until stiff peaks form. Gradually sprinkle sugar over, beating until sugar is dissolved and whites are glossy. Fold a large spoonful of whites into chocolate-cream mixture to lighten, then gently fold remaining whites and cream together until blended.

Spoon about one-third of the chocolate mixture into prepared tin, spreading it to the sides. Spoon the raspberries onto the chocolate half, spreading them evenly over the chocolate. Spoon in another third of the chocolate mixture, spreading it evenly. Top with remaining raspberries and cover completely with remaining chocolate mixture, smoothing the top evenly. Refrigerate 4–5 hours or overnight.

To serve, remove side of tin from charlotte. If necessary, use a thin-bladed knife to run between sponge fingers and side of tin. Transfer to a dessert plate.

Spoon whipped cream into a medium piping bag fitted with a medium star nozzle. Pipe a circle of scrolls or rosettes around edge of charlotte close to sponge fingers. Garnish centre of the charlotte with fresh raspberries and, if you like, tie a ribbon around finished dessert.

PEACHES N' WHITE CHOCOLATE CREAM MERINGUES

8 SERVINGS

MERINGUE SHELLS
3 egg whites
1.5 ml/¼ tsp cream of tartar
175 g/6 oz caster sugar
5 ml/1 tsp vanilla essence

POACHED PEACHES
100 g/4 oz sugar
½ cinnamon stick
2 strips zest from 1 lemon
750 ml/1¼ pts water
4 large peaches, just ripe

WHITE CHOCOLATE CREAM
100 g/4 oz good quality white
**   chocolate, chopped**
120 ml/4 fl oz milk
15 g/½ oz unsalted butter, cut into
**   pieces**
15 ml/1 tbsp vanilla essence or apricot
**   brandy**
250 ml/8 fl oz double cream
lemon zest and mint leaves for
decoration

Into a saucepan just large enough to hold the peaches, bring sugar, cinnamon stick, lemon zest and water to the boil; there should be enough liquid to cover peaches. Reduce heat.

Bring another saucepan about three-quarters full of water to the boil. Dip peaches into boiling water for 15–20 seconds, depending on ripeness. Transfer peaches to a bowl of ice water to cool. Remove from water and, using a small knife, carefully peel off skins. Alternatively, use a swivel-bladed vegetable peeler to peel peaches. Cut peaches in half lengthwise and, using a teaspoon, remove stones.

Drop peach halves into syrup and simmer 8–10 minutes, just until tender. Remove pan from the heat, but leave peaches to cool completely in syrup. Transfer peaches to a large bowl. Bring syrup to a boil and reduce until slightly thickened, 10–12 minutes. Strain syrup over peaches. Cool, then refrigerate until chilled, 2–3 hours.

Prepare meringue shells. Preheat oven to 140°C/275°F/Gas Mark 1. Line a large baking sheet with non-stick parchment paper or foil.

In a bowl with electric mixer, beat whites and cream of tartar until stiff peaks form. Gradually sprinkle three-quarters of the sugar over, a little at a time, beating well after each addition until whites are stiff and glossy. Fold in remaining sugar and vanilla.

Spoon mixture into a large piping bag fitted with a medium star nozzle. Pipe eight 7.5 cm/3 in circles about 4 cm/1½ in apart onto baking sheet. Pipe small rosettes in a ring around edge of each circle.

Bake 40–45 minutes, until set but not brown. Turn off oven and leave meringues in oven 45 minutes longer to dry out completely. Remove to wire rack to cool 10 minutes on baking sheet. Then

remove meringues from paper or foil to rack to cool completely. Store in an airtight container if not using at once.

Prepare white chocolate cream. In a saucepan over low heat, melt white chocolate with milk, stirring frequently until smooth. Remove from heat and stir in butter and vanilla. Chill 1 hour.

With electric mixer, beat cream until soft peaks form; do not overbeat or mixture will be too firm. Stir 1 spoonful of cream into chocolate mixture to lighten, then fold in remaining cream. Chill until firm, about 1 hour.

Arrange meringue shells on a serving dish or individual plates. Fill each shell with white chocolate cream. Remove peaches from their syrup and pat dry with paper towels. Cut each peach half into thin slices and arrange over white chocolate cream. Decorate with lemon zest and mint leaves. Spoon a little syrup onto each plate or serve separately.

VELVETY CHOCOLATE MOUSSE

6 SERVINGS

Traditional chocolate mousse like the one found in little French bistros does not contain cream. I use it here to give the very dark, plain chocolate an extra creamy texture — like velvet.

225 g/8 oz bittersweet chocolate, chopped
30 ml/2 tbsp orange-flavoured liqueur or brandy
60 ml/2 fl oz water
25 g/1 oz unsalted butter, cut into pieces
3 eggs, separated
1.5 ml/¼ tsp cream of tartar
50 g/2 oz sugar
120 ml/4 fl oz whipping cream
whipping cream for decoration
orange slices for decoration

In a saucepan over low heat, melt chocolate with orange-flavoured liqueur and water, stirring frequently until smooth. Remove from heat and beat in butter.

In a bowl, beat egg yolks until well blended. Beat into melted chocolate. Cool to room temperature.

With electric mixer, beat egg whites and cream of tartar until soft peaks form. Beat in sugar, 15 ml/1 tbsp at a time, beating well after each addition, until glossy but not too stiff or dry. Fold 1 large spoonful of whites into chocolate mixture to lighten.

In another bowl, whip cream until soft peaks form. Spoon cream over chocolate mixture and remaining whites over cream. Gently fold into chocolate just until blended. Pour into a serving bowl or into 6 individual dessert dishes and refrigerate at least 3 hours before serving. Decorate with whipped cream and orange slices.

SWEET SUCCESS

Leave the chocolate mixture to cool sufficiently before adding the egg whites so that heat of the chocolate does not deflate the whites. Do not overfold the whites; it does not matter if a few white streaks remain.

VELVETY CHOCOLATE MOUSSE ▶

CHOCOLATE BOX WITH WHITE CHOCOLATE MOUSSE AND BERRIES

8 SERVINGS

This dramatic dessert is much easier to make than it looks. The chocolate box can be made ahead and filled with any mousse; top with seasonal berries for a spectacular presentation.

CHOCOLATE BOX
175 g/6 oz plain chocolate, chopped
5 ml/1 tsp vegetable fat

WHITE CHOCOLATE MOUSSE
225 g/8 oz good quality white chocolate, chopped
60 ml/2 fl oz milk
30 ml/2 tbsp cherry or orange-flavoured liqueur
350 ml/12 fl oz double cream
2–3 egg whites, at room temperature
1.5 ml/¼ tsp cream of tartar

BERRY TOPPING
250 ml/8 fl oz double cream (optional)
675 g/1½ lbs strawberries, cut in half or other mixed berries
fresh mint sprigs for decoration

Turn a 23 cm/9 in square cake tin upside down. Place a piece of foil over pan and press against bottom and sides of tin to make a square shape. Carefully remove foil from tin, turn tin right-side up and line tin with moulded foil. Press foil against bottom and sides of tin smoothing out any wrinkles and folding any excess foil around tin edges.

In the top of a double boiler over low heat, melt chocolate and vegetable fat, stirring frequently, until smooth. Pour onto the foil-lined tin and gently tilt tin to coat bottom and sides evenly. Refrigerate tin 1 minute, then swirl any remaining chocolate up sides of tin to reinforce sides of chocolate box. Refrigerate 30–40 minutes, until completely set.

Prepare mousse. In a saucepan over medium heat, melt chocolate with milk, stirring frequently until smooth. Remove from heat and stir in liqueur. Cool to room temperature.

With electric mixer, beat cream until soft peaks form, do not overwhip or the mousse will be too stiff. Stir half the cream into chocolate to lighten, then fold in remaining cream.

In a bowl with electric mixer and clean beaters, beat egg whites and cream of tartar until stiff peaks form. Fold into chocolate-cream mixture.

Remove chocolate box in foil from tin using foil as a guide. Gently peel foil from sides and base and place box on a serving plate. Spoon mousse into the box and spread evenly. Chill until firm, 2–3 hours.

Prepare topping. In a bowl with an electric mixer, beat cream until it forms soft peaks. Spoon into a large piping bag fitted with a large star nozzle. Pipe a 2.5 cm/1 in border in a scroll or rosette pattern along sides of box. Fill centre with strawberries, raspberries or mixed berries and decorate with mint sprigs.

FRUIT-STUDDED CHOCOLATE MARQUISE WITH BOURBON CUSTARD CREAM

12 TO 14 SERVINGS

Dried fruits such as sultanas, apricots and prunes go so well with chocolate it was impossible to choose just one. This recipe combines three fruits in a dense, dark chocolate marquise mixture. This can be made several days ahead and stored in the refrigerator or even frozen.

50 g/2 oz sultanas
50 g/2 oz chopped, stoned prunes
40 g/1 ½ oz chopped, dried apricots
90 ml/3 fl oz bourbon, whisky or
　apricot brandy
350 g/12 oz plain chocolate, chopped
225 g/8 oz unsalted butter, cut into
　pieces
4 eggs, separated
1.5 ml/¼ tsp cream of tartar

BOURBON CUSTARD CREAM
475 ml/16 fl oz half cream
2 large eggs
100 g/4 oz sugar
30 ml/2 tbsp bourbon, whisky or
　apricot brandy

In a bowl, mix all the dried fruit with bourbon. Leave to stand at least 2 hours, stirring occasionally.

Line a 23 × 12.5 cm/9 × 5 in loaf tin with plastic wrap, allowing enough wrap to fold over bottom when marquise is finished.

In a saucepan over low heat, melt chocolate and butter, stirring frequently until smooth. In a bowl with hand-held electric mixer, beat egg yolks until pale and thick, 3–4 minutes. Stir into warm chocolate mixture and cook over low heat 1 minute, stirring constantly until mixture thickens and looks shiny. Remove from heat and cool, stirring occasionally. Stir in fruit and any remaining bourbon.

With electric mixer, beat egg whites and cream of tartar until stiff peaks

form; do not overbeat. Stir 1 large spoonful of whites into chocolate mixture to lighten, then fold in remaining whites.

Spoon into the pan. Chill just until firm, then fold over excess plastic wrap to cover the marquise. Refrigerate at least 6 hours or overnight.

Prepare bourbon cream. In a saucepan over medium heat, bring the half cream to the boil. Remove from heat. In a bowl, beat the eggs and sugar until well blended, about 1 minute.

Pour hot milk over and return mixture to saucepan over low heat. Cook 4–5 minutes, stirring constantly with a wooden spoon until mixture thickens and just coats the back of the spoon; do not boil or sauce will curdle. Strain into a chilled bowl and stir in bourbon. Refrigerate until ready to use.

To serve, slide marquise and its base onto a rectangular serving dish. Refrigerate until ready to serve. Cut into thin slices and serve with bourbon custard cream.

FRUITED WHITE CHOCOLATE BAVARIAN CREAMS WITH PASSION FRUIT AND CHOCOLATE SAUCES

8 SERVINGS

This gelatine-set white chocolate custard is made in heart-shaped moulds for an effective presentation. It can be made easily in ramekins or in a larger pretty mould. Vary the fruits according to the season.

vegetable oil for moulds
325 ml/11 fl oz whipping cream
100 g/4 oz good quality white
   chocolate, chopped
10 ml/2 tsp powdered gelatine
60 ml/2 fl oz water
250 ml/16 fl oz milk
4 egg yolks
50 g/2 oz sugar
30 ml/2 tbsp orange-flavoured liqueur

PASSION FRUIT SAUCE
6 very ripe passion fruit
60 ml/2 fl oz orange juice
30 ml/2 tbsp sugar or to taste
5 ml/1 tsp cornflour, dissolved in
   5 ml/1 tsp water
15 ml/1 tbsp orange-flavoured liqueur

CHOCOLATE LIQUEUR SAUCE
225 g/8 oz bittersweet chocolate,
   chopped
50 g/2 oz unsalted butter, cut into
   pieces
175 ml/6 fl oz water
30—45 ml/2—3 tbsp
   chocolate-flavoured liqueur
grated chocolate for garnish
fresh mint sprigs

Lightly oil 8 heart-shaped or other moulds. In a saucepan over low heat, bring 150 ml/5 fl oz cream to the boil. Add the white chocolate all at once, stirring until smooth. Set aside.

Sprinkle gelatine over water in a bowl; leave to stand and soften.

In a saucepan over medium heat, bring milk to the boil. In a bowl with a hand-held electric mixer, beat egg yolks and sugar until thick and pale, 2–3 minutes. Reduce mixer to lowest speed, gradually beat in milk, then return custard mixture to saucepan.

Cook custard over medium heat, stirring constantly with a wooden spoon until mixture thickens and coats the back of the spoon; do not boil or custard will curdle. Remove from the heat and stir in softened gelatine until dissolved, then stir into chocolate mixture. Strain custard into a large chilled bowl. Stir in orange-flavoured liqueur and refrigerate about 20 minutes, until mixture begins to thicken.

In a bowl with electric mixer, beat remaining cream until soft peaks form. Gently fold into the thickening gelatine-custard mixture. Spoon an equal amount into each mould. Place moulds on baking sheet and refrigerate 2 hours, or until set. Cover all moulds with plastic wrap and refrigerate several hours.

Prepare passion fruit sauce. Halve passion fruit crosswise. Scoop juice and seeds into a saucepan. Stir in orange juice, sugar and dissolved cornflour. Bring to the boil, then simmer 1–2 minutes, until sauce thickens. Remove from heat; cool slightly. Stir in orange-flavoured liqueur. Pour into a sauceboat.

Prepare chocolate sauce. In a saucepan over medium heat, melt chocolate and butter with water, stirring frequently until smooth. Remove from heat and cool slightly. Stir in chocolate-flavoured liqueur and strain into a sauceboat.

To serve, unmould desserts onto plates at least 30 minutes before serving to soften slightly. Fill a pie dish with hot water. Run a knife around the edge of each mould and dip into the hot water for 5–7 seconds. Dry bottom of mould; quickly cover dessert with a plate. Invert mould onto plate giving a firm shake; carefully remove mould.

Spoon a little of each sauce around each heart-shaped Bavarian cream. Garnish with grated chocolate and decorate with fresh mint.

CHOCOLATE POTS DE CRÈME

8 SERVINGS

Use the darkest chocolate you can find for this classic French dessert of dark, creamy chocolate custard.

475 ml/16 fl oz milk
100 g/4 oz sugar
225 g/8 oz plain or bittersweet chocolate, chopped
15 ml/1 tbsp vanilla essence
30 ml/2 tbsp brandy or other liqueur
7 egg yolks
whipped cream, chopped pistachios and Chocolate Leaves (see Decorating with Chocolate) for decoration

Preheat oven to 170°C/325°F/Gas Mark 3.

In a saucepan over medium heat, bring milk and sugar to the boil. Add chocolate all at once, stirring frequently until melted and smooth. Stir in vanilla and brandy.

In a bowl, beat egg yolks lightly. Slowly beat in chocolate mixture until well blended. Strain custard into 2 l/3½ pt measuring jug or large pitcher.

Place eight 120 ml/4 fl oz *pots de crème* cups or ramekins into a shallow roasting tin. Pour an equal amount of custard into each cup. Pour enough hot water into the tin to come about halfway up side of cups.

Bake 30–35 minutes, until custard is just set. Shake pan slightly; centre of each custard should jiggle. Or, insert knife into side of 1 custard and knife should come out clean. Remove tin from oven and transfer cups from tin to heat-proof surface to cool completely.

Place cooled custards on a baking sheet and cover with plastic wrap. Refrigerate until well chilled. (The custards can be stored 2 days in the refrigerator.)

To serve, decorate the top of each custard with a dollop or rosette of whipped cream. Sprinkle each with chopped pistachios and a chocolate leaf.

FRENCH CHOCOLATE POTS DE CRÈME ▶

CHOCOLATE-GLAZED CHOCOLATE ZUCCOTTO

8 TO 10 SERVINGS

This Florentine dessert was traditionally made in a pumpkin-shaped mould; zuccotto means "little pumpkin," but it is easily done in a mixing bowl.

1 chocolate roulade sponge (p.14)
120 ml/4 fl oz Amaretto liqueur
450 g/1 lb ricotta or mascarpone cheese
100 g/4 oz sugar
475 ml/16 fl oz whipping cream
15 ml/1 tbsp vanilla essence
175 g/6 oz plain chocolate, melted
30 ml/2 tbsp slivered almonds, toasted and chopped
grated zest of 1 orange plus 30 ml/2 tbsp juice
4 Amaretti biscuits, broken into small pieces
50 g/2 oz candied fruit, chopped

CHOCOLATE GLAZE

50 g/2 oz butter
45 ml/3 tbsp golden syrup
100 g/4 oz plain chocolate, chopped
extra grated orange zest for decoration

Prepare chocolate roulade sponge as on page 14. Line a 3 l/5 pt glass bowl with plastic wrap, allowing enough wrap to fold over bottom when dessert is finished. Cut cake in half lengthwise. Cut each strip into triangle-shaped pieces. Sprinkle cake pieces with 45 ml/3 tbsp Amaretto liqueur and line bowl with cake pieces leaving no open spaces, pressing cake firmly against sides of bowl. Reserve remaining cake pieces to make bottom.

If using ricotta cheese, press cheese through a strainer into large bowl. (This is not necessary for mascarpone cheese.) With a hand-held electric mixer, beat cheese and sugar until smooth.

In another bowl, beat whipping cream with vanilla until soft peaks form. Fold a spoonful of cream into cheese mixture to lighten, then fold in remaining cream. Divide mixture in half. Into half, fold melted chocolate and almonds; set aside. Into second half of cheese mixture, fold in orange zest and juice, remaining Amaretto liqueur, Amaretti biscuits and candied fruits.

Spoon the cheese and Amaretti mixture into the cake-lined bowl, spreading it to form an even layer all around bowl. Spoon the chocolate mixture into the centre and smooth top. Cover top with the remaining cake pieces and fold over excess plastic wrap, pressing down lightly to create a flat bottom. Refrigerate 6–8 hours or overnight, until very firm.

Prepare glaze. In a saucepan over medium heat, melt butter, golden syrup and chocolate, stirring frequently until smooth. Cool slightly until mixture is thickened but still pourable.

Peel back plastic wrap from top of zuccotto and unmould onto a serving plate; remove plastic wrap. Pour over glaze, using a palette knife to spread glaze evenly and scraping excess off dish. Clean plate. Refrigerate 5 minutes, until chocolate is set. Cut strips of waxed paper into triangles and place over dessert about 4 cm/1½ in apart. Dust with cocoa or icing sugar. Decorate top with orange zest. Refrigerate until ready to serve.

Frozen Desserts

FROZEN PEANUT BUTTER-FUDGE TORTE

WHITE CHOCOLATE RASPBERRY RIPPLE ICE CREAM

EASY FROZEN CHOCOLATE-MINT SOUFFLE

CHOCOLATE FROZEN YOGURT

RICH CHOCOLATE ICE CREAM

MILK CHOCOLATE ICE MILK

CHOCOLATE AND PECAN PARFAIT

CHOCOLATE AND STRAWBERRY FROZEN DAQUOISE

CHOCOLATE AND ORANGE SORBET

FROZEN CHOCOLATE AND CHERRY MOUSSE RING

ROCKY ROAD ICE CREAM PIE WITH ROCKY ROAD SAUCE

DOUBLE CHOCOLATE RUM AND RAISIN BOMBE

FROZEN CHOCOLATE-COATED BANANA POPS

DOUBLE CHOCOLATE BROWNIE-BAKED ALASKA

FROZEN PEANUT BUTTER-FUDGE TORTE

Use store-bought ice cream to make this welcome summertime cooler. The combination of chocolate ice cream, peanut butter and fudge is a well-loved favourite.

CRUMB CRUST
225 g/8 oz chocolate digestive biscuits
75 g/3 oz dry-roasted peanuts, finely chopped and toasted
50 g/2 oz unsalted butter, melted

FUDGE FILLING
120 ml/4 fl oz double cream
45 ml/3 tbsp golden syrup
150 g/5 oz plain chocolate, chopped
15 ml/1 tbsp vanilla essence

ICE CREAM LAYER
1.8 l/3 pts good quality chocolate ice cream
100 g/4 oz dry-roasted peanuts, chopped and toasted
350 ml/12 fl oz smooth peanut butter
175 g/6 fl oz honey
250 ml/8 fl oz whipping cream
50 g/2 oz sugar
10 ml/2 tsp vanilla essence
chocolate-covered peanuts for decoration

Prepare crust. In a food processor, process chocolate biscuits and peanuts until fine crumbs form. Pour in melted butter and process just until blended. Pat onto bottom and sides of 23 cm/9 in springform tin.

Prepare filling. In a saucepan over medium heat, bring cream and golden syrup to the boil. Remove from the heat and add chocolate all at once, stirring until melted and smooth. Stir in vanilla. Set aside, stirring occasionally until slightly cooled. Pour into prepared tin. Cool completely while preparing ice cream mixture.

Soften the ice cream 15–20 minutes at room temperature or until spreadable. In a bowl, combine nuts, peanut butter and honey until well blended. Add

softened ice cream scoop by scoop and, using hand-held mixer on low speed, beat ice cream into the peanut butter mixture just until mixed; do not let ice cream melt completely.

Pour ice cream mixture into fudge-lined tin. Cover and freeze 4–6 hours or overnight until very firm.

Remove dessert from freezer and leave to soften 5 minutes at room temperature. Run a knife around edge of tin and remove side of tin.

With hand-held mixer, beat cream, sugar and vanilla just until stiff peaks

form. Spoon cream into medium piping bag fitted with medium star nozzle and pipe cream in attractive design on top of torte. Decorate with chocolate-covered peanuts.

SWEET SUCCESS

Torte can be prepared in 23–25 cm/ 9–10 in deep pie dish which does not require unmoulding, but a springform tin gives a straight side which looks attractive when side is removed.

WHITE CHOCOLATE RASPBERRY RIPPLE ICE CREAM

MAKES ABOUT 1 L / 1 ¾ PTS

This sweet, creamy white chocolate ice cream is perfectly balanced by the slight tartness of the raspberry swirl. Serve with the left over Raspberry Ripple Sauce.

250 ml/8 fl oz milk
475 ml/16 fl oz whipping cream
7 egg yolks
30 ml/2 tbsp sugar
225 g/8 oz good quality white
　chocolate, chopped

RASPBERRY RIPPLE SAUCE
225 g/8 oz package frozen raspberries,
　sprinkled with 30 ml/2 tbsp sugar
　then defrosted
10 ml/2 tsp golden syrup
15 ml/1 tbsp lemon juice
15 ml/1 tbsp cornflour, diluted in
　15 ml/1 tbsp water

Prepare sauce. Into a saucepan press raspberries and their syrup through a sieve. Add golden syrup, lemon juice and dissolved cornflour. Bring to the boil, stirring frequently, then simmer 2–3 minutes, until sauce is thickened and syrupy. Pour into a bowl and cool to room temperature. Refrigerate sauce while preparing ice cream.

In a saucepan, bring milk and 250 ml/8 fl oz cream to the boil. In a bowl with hand-held mixer, beat egg yolks and sugar until thick and creamy, 2–3 minutes. Gradually pour hot milk over yolks, then return mixture to saucepan.

Cook over medium heat until custard thickens and lightly coats the back of a wooden spoon, stirring constantly; do not let boil or custard will curdle.

Remove pan from heat and stir in chocolate until melted and smooth. Pour remaining cold cream into a large bowl. Strain custard into bowl with cream. Blend well and cool to room temperature. Refrigerate until cold. Transfer custard to an ice cream maker and freeze according to manufacturer's directions.

When mixture is frozen but still soft, transfer one-third of the ice cream to a bowl. Spoon over some of the raspberry ripple sauce in concentric circles. Cover with another third of the ice cream and then more raspberry sauce. Cover with the remaining ice cream and a little more raspberry sauce. With a knife or spoon, lightly marble raspberry sauce into the ice cream. Cover and freeze.

Leave ice cream to soften 20–30 minutes in the refrigerator before serving. Scoop into bowl and drizzle over some of the remaining raspberry sauce.

SWEET SUCCESS

Freeze ice cream in a soufflé dish or other attractive bowl rather than in a plastic container so it can be served directly at the table.

EASY FROZEN CHOCOLATE-MINT SOUFFLÉ

8 SERVINGS

This is a delicious dessert, rich yet light textured. The chocolate is flavoured with a mint liqueur. Make sure you have a tall enough space in the freezer.

250 g/9 oz plain chocolate, broken into
   pieces
475 ml/16 oz double cream
4 eggs, separated
45—60 ml/3—4 tbsp mint-flavoured
   liqueur or 15 ml/1 tbsp peppermint
   essence
1.5 ml/¼ tsp cream of tartar
50 g/2 oz sugar
grated chocolate for decoration

CHOCOLATE-DIPPED MINT LEAVES
20—24 fresh mint leaves
100 g/4 oz plain chocolate, chopped

Prepare chocolate-dipped leaves. Rinse mint leaves in cold water and pat dry with paper towels. Line a baking sheet with waxed paper.

In the top of a double boiler over low heat, melt chocolate, stirring frequently until smooth. Leave to cool to just below body temperature. Holding stem end, dip each mint leaf about halfway into chocolate, coating both sides, leaving excess chocolate to drip into bowl. Place coated leaves on baking sheet and refrigerate; these leaves can be prepared 1–2 days ahead and refrigerated.

Prepare collar for soufflé dish. Cut a piece of waxed paper or foil long enough to encircle the dish, allowing a 5 cm/2 in overlap. Fold paper or foil in half lengthwise and wrap around dish so collar extends about 7.5 cm/3 in above sides of dish. Secure paper or foil with tape or kitchen string. Lightly oil the paper collar; set dish aside.

Place chocolate in a food processor fitted with the metal blade or in a blender.

In a saucepan, bring cream to the boil. With food processor or blender running, slowly pour cream over choco-late. Continue processing or blending until smooth, scraping the side of the container once.

With the machine still running, add the egg yolks, 1 at a time, processing well after each addition until well blended; chocolate mixture will be thick and creamy. Scrape into a bowl and stir in liqueur. Cool to room temperature; chocolate mixture will thicken further.

With electric mixer, beat egg whites and cream of tartar just until stiff peaks form. Add sugar, 30 ml/2 tbsp at a time, and continue beating just until whites are stiff and glossy; do not overbeat.

Stir 1 large spoonful of whites into chocolate mixture to lighten, then gently fold in remaining whites. Pour into the dish and freeze overnight. (Soufflé can be prepared 2–3 days ahead.)

To serve, remove tape or string from sides of dish and, using a knife as a guide, carefully unwrap paper from dish and soufflé. Press grated chocolate onto side of soufflé and top with a few choco-late-coated mint leaves. Serve remaining leaves with each portion of soufflé.

SWEET SUCCESS

To ensure a "well-risen" soufflé, choose a tall, narrow soufflé dish not more than 12.5–15 cm/5–6 in in diameter or soufflé mixture will not reach above edge of dish.

CHOCOLATE FROZEN YOGURT

This dark, chocolate frozen yogurt is so creamy and delicious it's hard to believe it is so easy to make. Not only that — it is a dieter's answer to prayers — low fat!

1.2 l/2 pts plain low fat yogurt
300 g/11 oz sugar
75 g/3 oz cocoa powder
15 ml/1 tbsp skinned milk powder, dissolved in 15–30 ml/1–2 tbsp milk or water

In a bowl with a wire whisk, mix together yogurt, sugar, cocoa and dissolved skimmed milk powder until smooth and well blended and sugar is dissolved. Refrigerate 1 hour, until cold.

Transfer yogurt mixture to an ice cream maker and freeze according to manufacturer's directions; this mixture will not freeze as hard as ice cream. Transfer to a freezerproof serving bowl or container and freeze 3–4 hours, until firm. (Frozen yogurt can be stored in the freezer 2–3 weeks in a freezer-proof container).

For mocha frozen yogurt, use coffee-flavoured low fat yogurt and add 15 ml/ 1 tbsp instant espresso or coffee powder, or experiment with other flavours.

RICH CHOCOLATE ICE CREAM

MAKES 1 ¼ QUARTS

This is a rich, smooth chocolaty ice cream, delicious on its own or as the basis for many variations.

225 g/8 oz plain chocolate, chopped
475 ml/16 fl oz half cream or milk
3 egg yolks
50 g/2 oz sugar
350 ml/12 fl oz double cream
15 ml/1 tbsp vanilla essence

In a saucepan over low heat, melt chocolate with 120 ml/4 fl oz half cream, stirring frequently until smooth. Remove from heat.

In a saucepan over medium heat, bring remaining half cream to the boil. In a bowl with hand-held mixer, beat egg yolks and sugar until thick and creamy, 2–3 minutes. Gradually pour hot milk over yolks, beating constantly, then return mixture to saucepan.

Cook over medium heat until custard thickens and lightly coats the back of a wooden spoon, stirring constantly; do not let mixture boil or custard will curdle. Immediately pour melted chocolate over, stirring constantly until well blended.

Pour cold cream into a bowl and strain custard into bowl with cream. Blend well and cool to room temperature. Refrigerate until cold.

Transfer custard to an ice cream maker and freeze according to manufacturer's directions. Leave to soften 15–20 minutes before serving.

VARIATIONS

White, Dark, or Milk Chocolate Chunk *— Stir 225 g/8 oz good quality white, dark, or milk chocolate, chopped, into ice cream when removing from ice cream machine.*

Mocha Ice Cream *— Prepare ice cream as directed but adding 30 ml/2 tbsp instant coffee or espresso powder, dissolved in 30 ml/2 tbsp water to melted chocolate before adding custard.*

MILK CHOCOLATE ICE MILK

This is the easiest "ice cream" ever. The high milk content in milk chocolate gives the ice milk a very creamy texture without added eggs or cream.

450 g/1 lb good quality milk chocolate, chopped
250 ml/8 fl oz half cream
475 ml/16 fl oz milk (not skimmed)
whipped cream for decoration

In a saucepan over low heat, melt chocolate with half cream, stirring frequently until smooth. Gradually stir in milk, beating until smooth and well-blended. Cook over low heat 5–7 minutes. Strain into a large bowl and cool to room temperature, stirring occasionally. Cover and refrigerate 6–8 hours or overnight.

If mixture has separated slightly, stir well. Transfer to an ice cream maker and freeze according to manufacturer's directions. Leave to soften 10–15 minutes at room temperature before serving. Serve decorated with whipped cream or chocolate sauce.

SWEET SUCCESS

If you do not have a sugar thermometer, you can test the temperature of the boiling caramel by pouring a few drops of caramel into a bowl of cold water; it should form into a soft ball when rolled between 2 fingers.

VARIATION

Mocha Milk Chocolate Ice Milk – *Prepare as above but add 30 ml/2 tbsp instant coffee or espresso powder dissolved in 30 ml/2 tbsp water to milk.*

CHOCOLATE AND PECAN PARFAIT

10 SERVINGS

A *parfait is a dessert mixture similar to a frozen mousse. This delicious chocolate mixture contains a surprise filling of pecan praline and chunks of milk chocolate.*

475 ml/16 fl oz double cream
250 g/9 oz plain chocolate, chopped
3 egg yolks
30 ml/2 tbsp almond- or hazelnut-
    flavoured liqueur
50 g/2 oz good quality milk chocolate,
    chopped into small pieces

PECAN PRALINE
vegetable oil for baking sheet
90 g/3½ oz pecan halves
225 g/8 oz sugar
60 ml/2 fl oz water
**Chocolate Curls (see Decorating with
    Chocolate) for decoration**

Prepare praline. Preheat oven to 180°C/350°F/Gas Mark 4. Oil a baking sheet and set aside. Spread pecan halves onto another baking sheet and bake 10–12 minutes, until pecans are well toasted.

In a saucepan over medium heat, heat sugar and water until the sugar dissolves, swirling the pan occasionally. Leave sugar to come to the boil and continue boiling until sugar turns a golden caramel colour. Stir in toasted pecans, then pour mixture onto the oiled baking sheet to cool and harden. Do not touch as caramel can stick and cause serious burns.

Leave praline to cool to room temperature. When hard, place in a deep bowl and crush with the end of a rolling pin or place in a heavy plastic bag and crush with a rolling pin. Set aside.

Line 20 × 10 cm/8 × 4 in loaf tin with plastic wrap, allowing enough wrap to fold over bottom when parfait is finished.

In a saucepan over medium heat, bring 250 ml/8 fl oz cream to the boil. Remove from the heat and add the chocolate all at once, stirring until melted and smooth. Add egg yolks, 1 at a time,

beating well after each addition. Strain into a bowl and stir in the liqueur. Set aside to cool and thicken.

In a bowl, beat remaining cream until soft peaks form; do not overbeat or cream will not blend into the chocolate mixture. Stir 1 spoonful cream into chocolate mixture to lighten, then fold in remaining cream just until blended.

Spoon one-third of the chocolate mixture into bottom of loaf tin, spreading evenly. Sprinkle one-quarter of the praline over and then one half of the milk chocolate. Spoon another third of the chocolate mixture over, spreading

to cover praline and chocolate. Sprinkle another quarter of the praline mixture and remaining milk chocolate over; spread with remaining chocolate mixture, smoothing top evenly. Fold over excess plastic wrap to cover parfait. Freeze 6–8 hours or overnight.

To serve, peel back plastic wrap from the top of the parfait. Invert onto serving plate and remove plastic wrap. Press remaining crushed praline onto sides of parfait and sprinkle a little on the top. Decorate top with chocolate curls. Leave parfait to soften about 30 minutes in the refrigerator before cutting into thin slices.

CHOCOLATE AND STRAWBERRY FROZEN DAQUOISE

10 SERVINGS

Meringue freezes beautifully, so this is an ideal dessert to make ahead and store in the freezer. Leave the daquoise to soften about 30 minutes in the refrigerator before serving.

275 g/10 oz sugar
30 ml/2 tbsp cocoa powder, sifted
5 egg whites
1.5 ml/¼ tsp cream of tartar
600 ml/1 pt good quality chocolate ice cream
600 ml/1 pt good quality strawberry ice cream
350 g/12 oz fresh strawberries
475 ml/16 fl oz whipping cream
50 g/2 oz sugar
30 ml/2 tbsp raspberry-flavoured liqueur

STRAWBERRY SAUCE
450 g/1 lb frozen strawberries, drained
15 ml/1 tbsp lemon juice
10 Chocolate-dipped Strawberries (p105) for decoration

CHOCOLATE-STRAWBERRY FROZEN DAQUOISE ▶

Preheat oven to 140°C/275°F/Gas Mark 1. Line 1 large and 1 small baking sheet with non-stick parchment paper or foil. Using 20 cm/8 in cake tin or plate as a guide, mark 2 circles on the large baking sheet and 1 circle on the small baking sheet.

In a bowl, mix together 50 g/2 oz sugar and the cocoa powder. Set aside.

With electric mixer, beat egg whites and cream of tartar until stiff peaks form. Gradually sprinkle remaining sugar over, a little at a time, beating well after each addition, until whites are stiff and glossy. Gently fold in cocoa and sugar mixture just until blended.

Spoon one-third of the meringue mixture inside each marked circle on baking sheets. Spread each meringue out evenly to 20 cm/8 in circle, smoothing tops and edges.

Bake meringues 1¼ hours, until crisp and dry. Transfer to wire racks to cool 10 minutes on baking sheets. Then remove meringues from parchment paper or foil to cool completely; meringues can be stored in an airtight container if not using at once.

Place meringue layers on a freezer-proof serving plate and freeze for 20 minutes; this makes them firmer and easier to handle while spreading ice cream. Meanwhile, remove chocolate and strawberry ice creams from freezer to soften 15–20 minutes.

Remove meringue layers and serving plate from freezer. Place 1 meringue layer on the plate and spread with chocolate ice cream to within 1 cm/½ in of edge. Cover with a second meringue layer and spread with strawberry ice cream to within 1 cm/½ in of edge. Top with third meringue layer, pressing layers gently together. Return to freezer 5–6 hours or overnight.

In a bowl with hand-held mixer, beat cream, sugar and raspberry liqueur until soft peaks form. Remove meringue layers from the freezer and spread top and side with cream in a swirling or decorative pattern. Freeze until ready to serve if not using at once.

For the sauce, process strawberries in a food processor with metal blade attached, until well blended. Press purée through a sieve into a bowl. Stir in lemon juice and if sauce is too thick, thin with a little water.

To serve, slice fresh strawberries lengthwise and decorate top of daquoise. Serve each slice with some strawberry sauce and a chocolate-dipped strawberry.

CHOCOLATE AND ORANGE SORBET

MAKES 1.75 L/3 PTS

A sorbet can be made with a fruit purée and a sugar syrup or with milk. Milk gives this dark sorbet a rich, velvety texture.

100 g/4 oz bittersweet chocolate, chopped
475 ml/16 fl oz milk
275 g/10 oz sugar
75 g/3 oz cocoa powder
175 g/6 oz container frozen orange juice concentrate, thawed

In a saucepan over low heat, melt chocolate with 120 ml/4 fl oz milk, stirring frequently until smooth. Set aside to cool.

In a bowl, combine sugar and cocoa powder. Make a well in centre of the mixture and, with a wire whisk, gradually stir in remaining milk, bringing in more and more of the cocoa mixture until all the cocoa and milk mixture is smooth. Beat in orange juice concentrate and orange zest.

Slowly beat cocoa and milk into melted chocolate until well blended. Refrigerate at least 1 hour, until cold.

Transfer mixture to an ice cream maker and freeze according to manufacturer's directions; this mixture will not freeze as hard as ice cream. Transfer to a serving bowl or container and freeze 3–4 hours, until firm. (Sorbet can be stored in the freezer 2–3 weeks in a freezerproof container).

FROZEN CHOCOLATE AND CHERRY MOUSSE RING

8 SERVINGS

This simple chocolate mousse is served with a fresh cherry sauce and garnished with Chocolate-dipped Cherries. The same sauce is delicious with Rich Chocolate Ice Cream.

225 g/8 oz plain chocolate, chopped
30 ml/2 tbsp cherry-flavoured liqueur
30 ml/2 tbsp water
4 eggs, separated
1.5 ml/¼ tsp cream of tartar
50 g/2 oz sugar
175 ml/6 fl oz whipping cream

POACHED CHERRIES
900 g/2 lbs fresh sweet cherries
1 orange
100 g/4 oz sugar
450 g/1 lb sugar
120 ml/4 fl oz seedless raspberry jam
   or redcurrant jelly
15 ml/1 tbsp cornflour, dissolved in
   15 ml/1 tbsp cold water
250 ml/8 fl oz whipping cream
15 ml/1 tbsp sugar
15 ml/1 tbsp cherry-flavoured liqueur
fresh mint leaves and Chocolate-
   dipped Cherries (see Double
   Chocolate-Dipped Fruit in Sweets
   chapter)

Lightly oil a 1.1 1/2 pt freezerproof ring or other mould. In a saucepan over low heat, melt chocolate with cherry-flavoured liqueur and water, stirring frequently until smooth. Remove from heat and beat in egg yolks, 1 at a time, beating well after each addition.

With electric mixer, beat whites and cream of tartar until soft peaks form. Gradually add sugar, 15 ml/1 tbsp at a time, beating well after each addition, until white are stiff and glossy but not dry. Fold a spoonful of whites into chocolate mixture to lighten, then fold in remaining chocolate.

With hand-held electric mixer, beat cream just until soft peaks form. Fold into chocolate mixture, then pour mousse into the prepared mould. Cover mould with plastic wrap and freeze 6–8

hours or overnight. (Mousse can be stored covered in the freezer for 1–2 days.)

Prepare cherries. Remove stems and using a cherry stoner or small knife, remove stones. Using a swivel-bladed vegetable peeler, remove zest from orange and squeeze juice. Place in a saucepan with sugar and water. Bring to the boil, then reduce heat. Add cherries to poaching liquid and simmer 7–10 minutes, until tender. Remove from heat and leave cherries in poaching liquid 3–4 hours.

Using a slotted spoon, transfer cherries from liquid to a bowl. Add raspberry jam and dissolved cornflour to syrup and bring to the boil, then reduce heat and simmer 1–2 minutes until syrup is thickened and coats the back of a spoon. Strain over cherries and cool to room temperature. Refrigerate until completely chilled.

To unmould mousse, run a thin-bladed knife around outer and inner edges of mould. Dip mould into warm water to come about halfway up sides of mould 5 seconds. Dry bottom of mould; quickly cover with serving plate. Invert mould onto plate, giving a firm shake; remove mould. Smooth surface with palette knife and return to freezer for 5 minutes to chill surface.

To serve, beat cream, sugar and cherry-flavoured liqueur until soft peaks form. Spoon one-quarter of cream into a small piping bag fitted with a medium star nozzle and pipe a decorative border around edge of mould; spoon remaining cream into centre of mould. Decorate outer edge with mint leaves and chocolate-dipped cherries and serve cherries in their sauce separately.

ROCKY ROAD ICE CREAM PIE WITH ROCKY ROAD SAUCE

10 SERVINGS

The combination of chocolate marshmallows and pecans is a classic one. This pie uses a soft-cocoa fudge between the ice cream layers and a chocolaty, marshmallow sauce over it!

CRUMB CRUST

225 g/8 oz chocolate digestive biscuits
40 g/1½ oz pecans, chopped and
    toasted
50 g/2 oz unsalted butter, melted

COCOA FUDGE

175 g/6 oz sugar
30 ml/2 tbsp cocoa powder
15 ml/1 tbsp golden syrup
120 ml/4 fl oz whipping cream
15 g/½ oz butter
1.2 1/2 pts chocolate ice cream
150 g/5 oz marshmallows, chopped
250 ml/8 fl oz whipping cream
175g /6 oz sugar
5 ml/1 tsp vanilla essence

ROCKY ROAD SAUCE

50 g/2 oz plain chocolate, chopped
mini-marshmallows
75 ml/2½ fl oz whipping cream
75 ml/2½ fl oz honey
Chocolate-dipped Pecan Halves (p9) *or*
    chopped pecans for decoration

Preheat oven to 200°C/400°F/Gas Mark 6. In a food processor, process chocolate biscuits and pecans until fine crumbs form. Pour in melted butter and process just until blended. Press onto bottom and sides of 23 cm/9 in pie dish, 4 cm/1½ in deep.

Bake piecrust 6–8 minutes, until set. Cool on wire rack completely. Freeze piecrust 20 minutes while preparing ice cream. Soften 600 ml/20 fl oz ice cream 15–20 minutes at room temperature. Spread ice cream onto bottom of frozen crust, smoothing surface evenly. Return to freezer until completely firm.

In a saucepan over medium heat, bring sugar, cocoa, golden syrup, cream and butter to the boil, stirring constantly until smooth. Remove from heat.

Remove pie dish from freezer and while cocoa fudge is still warm, pour over ice cream layer. Immediately sprinkle marshmallow pieces over, pressing them into the fudge layer with the back of a spoon, so warm fudge melts them slightly. Return pie to freezer, 25–30 minutes.

Soften remaining ice cream 20 minutes at room temperature. Remove pie from freezer and spread ice cream over fudge layer, spreading ice cream to edge of crust and covering completely. Return pie to freezer and freeze 4–6 hours or overnight.

With hand-held electric mixer, beat cream, sugar and vanilla just until stiff peaks form. Spread cream over pie to edge of crust in a swirling pattern and decorate with chocolate-dipped pecans or sprinkle with chopped pecans.

Leave pie to soften 30 minutes in refrigerator or 20 minutes at room temperature before serving. (Pie can be prepared up to 1 week ahead and stored in freezer.)

Prepare sauce. In a heavy-bottomed saucepan over low heat, melt chocolate and marshmallows with cream and honey, stirring frequently until smooth and well blended. Pour into sauceboat and serve warm poured over slices of ice cream pie.

DOUBLE CHOCOLATE RUM AND RAISIN BOMBE

10 SERVINGS

This rich, raisin-studded chocolate ice cream dessert contains a soft centre of white chocolate mousse. Garnish with Chocolate-dipped Prunes if you like.

CHOCOLATE RUM AND RAISIN ICE CREAM

75 g/3 oz raisins
135 ml/4½ fl oz light rum
175 g/6 oz plain chocolate, chopped
325 ml/11 fl oz milk
3 egg yolks
30 ml/2 tbsp sugar
60 ml/2 fl oz honey
250 ml/8 fl oz whipping cream

WHITE CHOCOLATE MOUSSE

75 g/3 oz sultanas
45 ml/3 tbsp light rum
250 ml/8 fl oz whipping cream
150 g/5 oz good quality white chocolate, chopped
2 egg whites
1.5 ml/¼ tsp cream of tartar
50 g/2 oz sugar
30 ml/2 tbsp sugar
15 ml/1 tbsp cocoa powder
15 ml/1 tbsp light rum
120 ml/4 fl oz whipping cream
10 Chocolate-dipped Prunes (see recipe in Sweets chapter)

In a bowl, mix raisins and 60 ml/2 fl oz rum. Leave to stand at least 2 hours, stirring occasionally.

In a saucepan over low heat, melt both chocolates with 75 ml/2½ fl oz milk, stirring frequently until smooth. Set aside.

In another saucepan, bring remaining 250 ml/8 fl oz milk to the boil. In a bowl with hand-held mixer, beat egg yolks with the sugar and honey until pale and thick, about 2 minutes. Pour about 250 ml/8 fl oz hot milk over the yolks and return the mixture to the pan.

Cook egg-and-milk custard over low heat until mixture thickens and lightly coats the back of a spoon, stirring constantly, 5–7 minutes. Stir hot custard into the melted chocolate mixture until well blended.

Place the cold cream in a large bowl and strain hot chocolate custard mixture over – beat together until well blended; cold cream stops the custard cooking. Stir in remaining 15 ml/1 tbsp rum and leave to cool, stirring occasionally. Refrigerate 2–3 hours until well chilled.

Transfer custard to an ice cream maker and freeze according to manufacturer's directions. Transfer to a large bowl and stir in rum-soaked raisins, then freeze until firm, at least 2 hours.

Chill a 1.75 l/3 pt ice cream bombe mould or freezerproof glass mixing bowl in the freezer. Remove ice cream from freezer to soften at room temperature, about 15 minutes. When bowl is chilled and ice cream softened, spread ice cream in an even layer on base and up sides of chilled mould or bowl using the back of a spoon to smooth. Return to freezer.

Prepare mousse. In a small bowl, mix raisins and 60 ml/2 fl oz rum. Leave to stand at least 2 hours, stirring occasionally.

In a saucepan over low heat, bring 15 ml/1 tbsp cream to the boil. Remove from heat and stir in chocolate all at once until melted and smooth. Stir in remaining 15 ml/1 tbsp rum and rum-soaked raisins and set aside to cool.

With electric mixer, beat egg whites and cream of tartar until stiff peaks form. Sprinkle sugar over, 15 ml/1 tbsp at a time, beating well after each addition, until whites are stiff and glossy. Stir 1 spoonful of whites into melted chocolate mixture to lighten, then fold in remaining whites.

In another bowl with hand-held electric mixer, beat remaining whipping cream until soft peaks form. Fold in mousse mixture, then fold in soaked raisins.

Remove ice cream-lined bombe or bowl from freezer and fill with the white chocolate mousse. Cover and freeze 6–8 hours or overnight. (Bombe can be prepared 1 week ahead and stored in freezer.)

Remove bombe from freezer and uncover. Dip a thin-bladed knife into hot water and dry. Quickly run knife around sides of mould to loosen ice cream. Dip mould or bowl into warm water, about halfway up sides of mould, about 5 seconds. Dry mould and run knife or spatula around side again until bombe is released. Set a serving plate over mould and invert mould onto plate with a firm shake. Smooth surface and return to freezer to set surface.

Stir together sugar and cocoa, making a well in centre. Slowly stir in cream until sugar and cocoa are well dissolved. Add the rum and, with a hand-held mixer, beat cream just until stiff peaks form; do not overbeat.

Spoon cocoa-flavoured cream into small piping bag fitted with a medium star nozzle. Pipe a swirl of cream around edge of mould and decorate with the Chocolate-dipped Prunes. If you like, pipe a few rosettes around top edge or 1 rosette in centre. Leave bombe to soften 10–15 minutes at room temperature or 20–30 minutes in refrigerator.

FROZEN CHOCOLATE-COATED BANANA POPS

6 SERVINGS

All children love banana and these chocolate-coated bananas on a stick are special favourites all year round. Cut and freeze extra bananas any time and they'll be ready for coating at a moments notice.

3 bananas, unbruised and fully ripe
225 g/8 oz plain chocolate, chopped
45 ml/3 tbsp white vegetable fat
75 g/3 oz unsalted peanuts, chopped

Line a small baking sheet with waxed paper. Peel bananas, being sure to remove all stringy fibres. Cut each in half crosswise, then insert a wooden lollipop stick 4 cm/1½ in into cut-end of each banana half. Place on lined baking sheet and freeze 3 hours or overnight, until very firm.

In a saucepan, melt chocolate and white vegetable fat, frequently until smooth. Pour into a tall mug or paper cup or other tall, narrow container. Leave chocolate to cool 10–15 minutes, until slightly thickened.

Spread peanuts onto a small flat plate or piece of waxed paper or foil. Hold 1 banana by the stick and dip into chocolate, tilting mug or cup and twisting banana until completely coated in chocolate. Quickly pull out banana and hold upright, then immediately roll in chopped nuts just until lightly coated.

Place on waxed paper-lined baking sheet and place in freezer to harden. Continue with each pop and place each on prepared baking sheet as soon as it is coated. Freeze at least 1 hour, until chocolate is completely hardened. (Pops can be stored covered in the freezer for 1–2 weeks – if they last that long!)

SWEET SUCCESS

Do not use metal sticks or small pointed wooden skewers as they could be harmful or cause injury to small children. Lollipop sticks are available in larger supermarkets.

DOUBLE CHOCOLATE BROWNIE-BAKED ALASKA

8 TO 10 SERVINGS

This frozen dessert is an ideal party piece as it can be prepared well ahead and stored in the freezer until ready for baking. Use homemade or good quality bought ice creams and any combination you like.

1 batch Rich Chocolate Ice Cream (p65) or 600 ml/1 pt good quality chocolate ice cream
1 batch White Chocolate-Raspberry Ripple Ice Cream (p62) or 600 ml/ 1 pt good quality vanilla ice cream
600 ml/1 pt good quality raspberry sorbet
4 egg whites, at room temperature
1.5 ml/¼ tsp cream of tartar
225 g/8 oz sugar
10 ml/2 tsp vanilla essence

BROWNIE LAYER

50 g/2 oz unsalted butter, cut into pieces
50 g/2 oz plain chocolate, chopped
75 g/3 oz sugar
2 eggs
5 ml/1 tsp vanilla essence
50 g/2 oz plain flour
40 g/1½ oz pecans, chopped and toasted
fresh raspberries for decoration

Prepare brownie layer. Preheat oven to 180°C/350°F/Gas Mark 4. Lightly grease and flour 20 cm/8 in cake tin.

In a saucepan over low heat, melt butter and chocolate, stirring frequently until smooth. Remove from heat and stir in sugar, eggs and vanilla and beat just until blended. Stir in flour and pecans just until blended. Spoon into tin.

Bake 25–30 minutes, until a slight indentation remains on top when touched lightly with a fingertip. Transfer to wire rack to cool to room temperature. Invert onto wire rack to cool completely. Wrap tightly in plastic wrap until ready to use.

Line a 1.5–2 1/2½–3½ pt freezer-proof mixing bowl with a flat bottom and diameter of not more than 20 cm/8 in with plastic wrap, allowing enough wrap to fold over bottom when dessert is finished.

Soften chocolate ice cream at room temperature 15–20 minutes or until it can be easily scooped. Spread the ice cream into an even 2.5 cm/1 in layer around the bowl to within 1 cm/½ in of top of bowl. Cover and freeze 15–20 minutes. Meanwhile, remove white chocolate ice cream from freezer to soften.

When white chocolate ice cream is soft enough to spread, remove chocolate ice cream-lined bowl from freezer. Spread white chocolate ice cream into an even layer against the chocolate layer, about 2.5 cm/1 in thick. Cover,

then re-freeze 15–20 minutes. Meanwhile, remove raspberry sorbet from freezer to soften.

Fill centre of bowl with raspberry sorbet and smooth the surface evenly. Place the brownie layer onto the surface of the ice cream-filled bowl and press against the surface; trim to fit if necessary. Fold plastic wrap over top of bowl and return to freezer at least 6 hours or overnight.

Peel back plastic wrap from top of bowl. Invert bowl onto an ovenproof serving plate. Remove plastic wrap from ice cream and return plate to freezer.

Preheat oven to 240°C/475°F/Gas Mark 9. With an electric mixer, beat whites and cream of tartar until stiff peaks form. Gradually add sugar, beating well after each addition, until peaks are stiff and glossy. Beat in vanilla.

Spread about 30 ml/2 tbsp meringue over top of dessert. Spoon remaining meringue into a large piping bag fitted with a medium star nozzle and pipe vertical stripes, with edges touching, around sides of moulded dessert. Be sure all edges around side of dessert and bottom are well sealed. Pipe a pretty border around edge of flat top of the dessert, making an edge to contain decoration. (Dessert can be frozen at this stage up to 1 hour ahead if necessary.)

Bake 3–5 minutes, until meringue is golden and set. Fill top of meringue with fresh raspberries and serve with raspberry sauce.

SWEET SUCCESS

If using White Chocolate Raspberry-Ripple Ice Cream and Rich Chocolate Ice Cream, you will not need all the ice cream each recipe yields, but it is impractical to make these ice creams in smaller quantities. Store any left over ice cream in small, freezerproof containers.

Biscuits and Brownies

CHOCOLATE CHUNK CHOCOLATE DROPS

CHOCOLATE "AMARETTI" BISCUITS

BITTERSWEET FUDGE BISCUITS

CHOCOLATE FEATHERED TUILES

CHOCOLATE-FILLED CIGARETTES RUSSES

CHOCOLATE CHIP AND PECAN SHORTBREAD

CHOCOLATE CHIP AND GINGER FLORENTINES

BRANDIED BROWNIE "TART"

CHOCOLATE VIENNESE BISCUITS

CHOCOLATE CRACKLE TOPS

CHOCOLATE AND HAZELNUT PINWHEELS

WHITE CHOCOLATE FRUIT 'N' NUT BARS

BLACK-AND-WHITE CHOCOLATE-MINT SANDWICH BISCUITS

CHUNKY CHOCOLATE BROWNIES WITH FUDGE GLAZE

CHOCOLATE AND PECAN MERINGUES

CHOCOLATE AND COCONUT SARAH BERNHARDTS

COCOA BROWNIES WITH
MILK CHOCOLATE AND WALNUT TOPPING

CREAM CHEESE-MARBLED BROWNIES

CHOCOLATE CHUNK CHOCOLATE DROPS

These are very big chocolate biscuits which are filled with chunks of chocolate and nuts. They are thin and crisp near the edges but soft and fudgy inside.

175 g/6oz plain chocolate, chopped

100 g/4 oz unsalted butter, cut into pieces

2 eggs

100 g/4 oz sugar

40 g/1½ oz brown sugar

40 g/1½ oz flour

25 g/1 oz cocoa powder

5 ml/1 tsp baking powder

10 ml/2 tsp vanilla essence

1.5 ml/¼ tsp salt

90 g/3½ oz pecans, toasted and chopped

175 g/6 oz plain chocolate chips

100 g/4 oz good quality white chocolate, chopped into 0.5 cm/¼ in pieces

100 g/4 oz good quality milk chocolate, chopped into 0.5 cm/¼ in pieces

Preheat oven to 170°C/325°F/Gas Mark 3. Grease 2 large baking sheets. In a medium saucepan over low heat, melt chocolate and butter, stirring frequently until smooth. Remove from heat to cool slightly.

With electric mixer, beat eggs and sugars until thick and pale, 2–3 minutes. Gradually pour in melted chocolate, beating until well blended. Beat in flour, cocoa powder, baking powder, vanilla and salt just until blended. Stir in nuts, chocolate chips and chocolate pieces.

Drop heaping tablespoonsful of dough, at least 10 cm/4 in apart, flattening dough slightly, trying to keep about a 7.5 cm/3 in circle; you will only get 4–6 biscuits on each sheet. Bake 10–12 minutes, until tops are cracked and shiny; do not overbake or they will break when removed from baking sheet.

Remove biscuits to wire rack to cool until firm, but not too crisp. Before they become too crisp, transfer each biscuit to wire rack to cool completely. Continue to bake in batches. Store biscuits in an airtight container.

If you need to use the same baking sheets to bake in batches, cool by running back of baking sheet under cold water and wiping surface with a paper towel before re-greasing.

CHOCOLATE "AMARETTI" BISCUITS

ABOUT 24

These chocolate-almond meringue cookies are based on the popular Italian Amaretti cookie. They are easy to make and are the ideal accompaniment to espresso coffee.

150 g/5 oz blanched whole almonds
100 g/4 oz caster sugar
15 ml/1 tbsp cocoa powder
30 ml/2 tbsp icing sugar
2 egg whites
pinch cream of tartar
5 ml/1 tsp almond essence
icing sugar for dusting

Preheat oven to 180°C/350°F/Gas Mark 4. Place almonds on a small baking sheet and bake 10–12 minutes, stirring occasionally, until golden brown. Remove from oven and cool to room temperature; reduce oven temperature to 170°C/325°F/Gas Mark 3. Line a large baking sheet with non-stick parchment paper or foil.

In a food processor fitted with the metal blade, process almonds with 50 g/2 oz sugar until almonds are finely ground, but not oily. Transfer to a bowl and sift in cocoa powder and icing sugar; stir to blend. Set aside.

With electric mixer, beat egg whites and cream of tartar until soft peaks form. Sprinkle in remaining sugar, 15 ml/ 1 tbsp at a time, beating well after each addition, until whites are glossy and stiff. Beat in almond essence.

Sprinkle almond sugar mixture over and gently fold into beaten whites just until blended. Spoon mixture into a large piping bag fitted with a medium, plain 1 cm/½ in nozzle. Pipe 4 cm/1½ in circles about 2.5 cm/1 in apart onto prepared baking sheet.

Bake 12–15 minutes, or until biscuits appear crisp. Transfer to wire rack to cool 10 minutes. With palette knife transfer biscuits to wire rack to cool completely. When cool, dust with icing sugar and store in an air-tight container.

SWEET SUCCESS

As an alternative decoration, lightly press a few coffee-sugar crystals onto top of each biscuit before baking.

BITTERSWEET FUDGE BISCUITS

MAKES 36

These chocolaty drop biscuits are easy to make, but the batter should be allowed to chill before handling. Firm on the outside, these biscuits are dark and fudgy on the inside. Use the best-quality chocolate you can find.

175 g/6 oz bittersweet chocolate, chopped

100 g/4 oz unsalted butter, at room temperature

100 g/4 oz sugar

2 eggs

5 ml/1 tsp vanilla essence

175 g/6 oz plain flour

2.5 ml/½ tsp salt

90 g/3½ oz pecans, chopped and toasted

75 g/3 oz good quality white chocolate, chopped into 0.5 cm/¼ in pieces

melted chocolate for decoration

In the top of a double boiler over low heat, melt chocolate, stirring frequently until smooth. Remove from heat.

With electric mixer, cream butter, sugar, eggs and vanilla until creamy and smooth, 2–3 minutes, scraping bowl occasionally. Slowly beat in the cooled chocolate until well blended.

Gradually stir in flour and salt, stirring just until blended. Stir in the pecans and chopped white chocolate. Cover bowl with plastic wrap and refrigerate 1 hour or until firm.

Meanwhile, preheat the oven to 190°C/375°F/Gas Mark 5. Lightly grease 2 large baking sheets. Drop rounded teaspoonsful of dough at least 5 cm/2 in apart onto the prepared baking sheets, flattening slightly; it may take 2 batches.

Bake 8–10 minutes, or just until surface feels slightly firm when touched with a fingertip. Remove baking sheets to wire racks to cool 5–7 minutes. With a palette knife, remove biscuits to wire rack to cool completely. Repeat with remaining dough. When cool, drizzle chocolate over them using a spoon. Store in airtight containers.

CHOCOLATE FEATHERED TUILES

MAKES 10–12

These wafer-thin biscuits are called tuiles in French because they resemble the roof tiles used on houses. They are the perfect biscuit to accompany ice creams, mousses and custard desserts. These have an added feather pattern which is fussy to make — but worth the effort!

1 egg white
50 g/2 oz caster sugar
30 ml/2 tbsp plain flour, sifted
2.5 ml/½ tsp vanilla essence
25 g/1 oz unsalted butter, melted
5 ml/1 tsp cocoa powder

Preheat oven to 190°C/375°F/Gas Mark 5. Generously grease 2 large baking sheets; you will need to work in batches.

With hand-held mixer, beat egg white just until stiff. Gradually beat in sugar, 15 ml/1 tbsp at a time, beating well after each addition, until the whites are glossy and stiff.

Fold sifted flour and vanilla into the egg whites, then fold in butter. Gently spoon about 30 ml/2 tbsp batter into a small bowl and fold cocoa into the smaller amount of batter. Spoon the cocoa batter into a small piping bag fitted with a small writing tip or a paper cone (see Decorating with Chocolate). Set aside.

Drop rounded teaspoonsful of plain batter, at least 7.5 cm/3 in apart, onto prepared baking sheets. Using the back of a spoon or palette knife spread out batter to about 7.5 cm/3 in in diameter.

Pipe 4 or 5 lines of cocoa batter cross-wise across each circle, then draw a skewer or cocktail stick lengthwise through lines in alternate directions to create a feather pattern.

Bake 4–5 minutes, until edges begin to turn brown and appear set. Using a palette knife, immediately lift each tuile from the baking sheet and place, top-side up, over a rolling pin to curl and

set; cool completely. If tuiles begin to harden before you have them over the rolling pin, return to oven 15–20 seconds to soften enough to remove without breaking. Continue in batches until all batter is used. (Store up to 2 days in an airtight container.)

SWEET SUCCESS

For chocolate tuiles, add the cocoa to all the plain batter and omit feathering process. Drape plain cooked tuiles over small juice glasses to create small tulip shapes to fill with ice cream, sorbet, mousse or custard desserts.

CHOCOLATE-FILLED CIGARETTES RUSSES

MAKES 10–12

These delicate, melt-in-the-mouth biscuits use Chocolate Feathered Tuiles. Rolled into cigarette shapes, they are then filled with a creamy, rich chocolate ganache.

Chocolate Feathered Tuiles (p80)

CHOCOLATE GANACHE
175 g/6 oz plain chocolate, chopped
120 ml/4 fl oz double cream
30 ml/2 tbsp Amaretto liqueur

Prepare ganache. In a medium saucepan over medium heat, bring cream to the boil. Add chocolate all at once, stirring until melted and smooth. Remove from heat and stir in Amaretto liqueur. Cool 2–3 hours, until thickened to piping consistency.

Meanwhile, prepare tuile batter, but substitute almond essence for the vanilla and add the cocoa to all the plain batter.

Bake tuiles as on p80. Remove tuiles from baking sheet and roll each around the handle of a wooden spoon or pencil. Press along edge to seal, then leave to set about 2 minutes. Continue shaping each biscuit until all biscuits are rolled into a cigarette shape. Cool as directed.

Spoon ganache into a medium piping bag fitted with a small writing nozzle; be sure nozzle can fit into each rolled biscuit. Pipe some ganache into each biscuit and set aside. Do not refrigerate or ganache will become too firm. Serve with ice cream or after-dinner coffee.

ALTERNATIVE DECORATION

Melt 50 g/2 oz plain chocolate in the top of a double boiler. In a cup, place 25 g/1oz chopped and toasted almonds.
If you like, dip one end of each biscuit into melted chocolate and then into chopped almonds. Place on waxed paper-lined baking sheet until set.

CHOCOLATE CHIP AND PECAN SHORTBREAD

MAKES 32 WEDGES

This is tender, melt-in-your-mouth shortbread. It is so simple to prepare, but the addition of ground pecans and chocolate chips makes a traditional biscuit more sophisticated.

90 g/3½ oz pecans, toasted and cooled
200 g/7 oz plain flour
25 g/1 oz cornflour
75 g/3 oz icing sugar
1.5 ml/¼ tsp salt
225 g/8 oz unsalted butter, softened
175 g/6 oz plain chocolate chips
40 g/1½ oz plain chocolate, melted, for drizzling

Preheat oven to 170°C/325°F/Gas Mark 3. In a food processor or blender, process the pecans until fine crumbs form; do not over-process nuts as the oil which is released can begin to form a paste.

Place in a large bowl with flour, cornflour, sugar and salt. Using a pastry blender or fingertips, cut or rub butter into flour mixture until well blended and mixture is almost creamy; do not let butter melt. Stir in chocolate chips.

Divide dough between 2 very lightly greased 20 cm/8 in tart tins or cake tins with removable bottoms and pat or spread evenly into tins. Bake 25–35 minutes, or until edges are golden and surface appears slightly puffy. Transfer tins to wire rack to cool 2–3 minutes.

Remove side of tins and place shortbread on heatproof surface. Cut each shortbread circle into 16 thin wedges; this must be done while shortbread is still hot and soft or it will crumble. Return shortbread wedges on their tin bases to wire rack to cool completely.

With palette knife, remove shortbread wedges to wire rack, alternating direction of wedges with every other one, wide edge, then pointed end up. Spoon melted chocolate into a small paper cone (see Decorating with Chocolate) and drizzle shortbread wedges evenly with chocolate. Leave chocolate to set. Store shortbread for 1 week in an airtight container.

SWEET SUCCESS

Dough can be blended with hand-held electric mixer at low speed, but do not overwork or baked shortbread may be tough or butter melt. Mixture can be baked in a 23 × 32.5 cm/9 × 13 in baking dish and cut into long fingers or squares, but the wedges with the crinkly edges from a tart tin look prettiest.

CHOCOLATE CHIP AND GINGER FLORENTINES

These deliciously chewy biscuits are named after the Italian city. This lacy version has lots of chopped ginger and is studded with tiny chocolate chips and glazed.

120 ml/4 fl oz double cream
50 g/2 oz unsalted butter
100 g/4 oz sugar
30 ml/2 tbsp honey
175 g/6 oz slivered almonds
75 ml/5 tbsp plain flour
2.5 ml/½ tsp ground ginger
50 g/2 oz diced candied orange peel
75 g/3 oz diced stem ginger
plain chocolate chips for sprinkling
225 g/8 oz bittersweet chocolate,
   chopped

Preheat oven to 180°C/350°F/Gas Mark 4. Lightly grease 2 large non-stick baking sheets or grease 2 baking sheets; non-stick baking sheets are ideal.

In a saucepan over medium heat, stir cream, butter, sugar and honey until sugar dissolves. Bring to the boil, stirring constantly. Remove from heat and stir in almonds, flour and ginger until well blended. Stir in orange peel and diced ginger.

Drop teaspoonful of mixture, at least 7.5 cm/3 in apart, onto prepared sheets. Spread each circle as thin as possible with the back of the spoon; dip spoon into water to prevent sticking. Sprinkle each with a few chocolate chips.

Bake 8–10 minutes, or until edges are golden brown and biscuits are bubbling. Do not underbake or biscuits will be sticky, but be careful not to overbake as the high sugar and fat content lets them burn easily.

Remove to wire rack to cool for 10 minutes, until firm. Using a palette knife, carefully transfer biscuits to wire rack to cool completely.

In top of a double boiler over low heat, melt chocolate, stirring frequently until smooth. Remove top of double boiler from bottom and cool about 5 minutes, stirring occasionally until slightly thickened.

Spread chocolate on flat side of each biscuit and place on wire rack, chocolate-side up. Refrigerate 2–3 minutes, until set. Using a serrated knife, fork or cake decorating comb, make wavy lines on chocolate layer. Refrigerate 10–15 minutes to set completely. (Biscuits can be refrigerated in an airtight container for 1 week.)

BRANDIED BROWNIE "TART"

This is a classic brownie – dense and chewy, made into a sophisticated dessert by the addition of brandy.

50 g/2 oz bittersweet chocolate, chopped
100 g/4 oz unsalted butter
75 g/3 oz sugar
2 eggs
30 ml/2 tbsp brandy
25 g/1 oz plain flour
50 g/2 oz pecans or walnuts, chopped and toasted
75 g/3 oz good quality white chocolate, chopped into 0.5 cm/¼ in pieces

CHOCOLATE-BRANDY GLAZE
60 ml/2 fl oz whipping cream
100 g/4 oz plain chocolate, chopped
30 ml/2 tbsp brandy
40 g/1½ oz pecans

Preheat oven to 170°C/325°F/Gas Mark 3. Generously grease a 23 cm/9 in tart tin. In a saucepan over low heat, melt chocolate and butter, stirring frequently until smooth. Remove from heat.

Stir in sugar and continue stirring 2 minutes longer, until sugar is dissolved. Beat in eggs and brandy. Stir in flour just until blended. Stir in nuts and chopped chocolate. Pour batter into tart tin, smoothing top evenly.

Bake 18–20 minutes, until edges are set and fine skewer or cocktail stick inserted 5 cm/2 in from the side of tin comes out with just a few crumbs attached. Transfer to wire rack to cool 30 minutes.

Prepare glaze. In a saucepan over medium heat, bring cream to the boil. Add chocolate all at once, stirring until smooth. Remove from heat; stir in brandy. Cool glaze 30 minutes, until thickened, but spreadable.

Remove side of tart tin and place brownie on wire rack over baking sheet to catch drips. Using a palette knife, spread glaze over top of brownie just to edges. Decorate the top with two rows of pecans. Leave to set, then transfer to serving plate and refrigerate 2–4 hours, until completely cold.

BRANDIED BROWNIE TART ▶

CHOCOLATE VIENNESE BISCUITS

This butter-rich, cocoa-flavoured biscuit looks stunning when piped into an "S" shape and dipped in dark chocolate.

275 g/10 oz plain flour
50 g/2 oz cocoa powder
45 ml/3 tbsp cornflour
225 g/8 oz unsalted butter, softened
75 g/3 oz icing sugar, sifted
100 g/4 oz plain chocolate, chopped
icing sugar for dusting

Preheat oven to 180°C/350°F/Gas Mark 4. Grease 2 large baking sheets. Into a bowl, sift together flour, cocoa powder and cornflour.

In another bowl with hand-held electric mixer, beat butter and sugar

2–3 minutes, until light and creamy. Slowly beat in the flour mixture in batches, just until blended.

Spoon dough into a large piping bag fitted with a large star nozzle. Pipe about twenty 7.5 cm/3 in fingers or "S" shapes about 5 cm/2 in apart onto baking sheets.

Bake 15–20 minutes, or until set. Remove to wire racks on baking sheets to cool 15 minutes. Using a palette knife, remove biscuits to wire rack to cool completely.

In the top of a double boiler over low heat, melt chocolate, stirring frequently until smooth. Pour into a bowl. Dip each end of biscuit into melted chocolate and place on a waxed paper-lined baking sheet to set. Cover chocolate-coated ends with a strip of waxed paper or foil and carefully dust the middle with icing sugar. Store in an airtight container.

CHOCOLATE CRACKLE TOPS

MAKES ABOUT 38

These are delicious, fudgy biscuits with a texture like a brownie. Once baked, the biscuit top cracks and the icing sugar creates a striking contrast to the chocolate interior.

200 g/7 oz plain chocolate, chopped
90 g/3½ oz unsalted butter
150 g/5 oz caster sugar
3 eggs
15 ml/1 tbsp vanilla essence
175 g/6 oz plain flour
25 g/1 oz cocoa powder
2.5 ml/½ tsp baking powder
1.5 ml/¼ tsp salt
175–225 g/6–8 oz icing sugar for
    coating

In a saucepan over low heat, melt chocolate and butter, stirring frequently until smooth. Remove from heat. Stir in sugar and continue stirring 2–3 minutes, until sugar dissolves. Add eggs, 1 at a time, beating well after each addition, then stir in vanilla.

Into a bowl, sift together flour, cocoa powder, baking powder and salt. Gradually stir into chocolate mixture in batches just until blended. Cover dough and refrigerate 2–3 hours or overnight, until dough is cold and holds its shape.

Preheat oven to 170°C/325°F/Gas Mark 3. Grease 2 or more large baking sheets. Place 150 g/5 oz icing sugar in a small, deep bowl. Using a small ice cream scoop, about 2.5 cm/1 in in diameter, or a teaspoon, scoop cold dough into small balls.

Between palms of hands, roll dough into 4 cm/1½ in balls. Drop balls, 1 at a time, into icing sugar and roll until heavily coated. Remove ball with a slotted spoon and tap against side of bowl to remove excess sugar. Place on baking sheets 4 cm/1½ in apart. Use more icing sugar as necessary; you may need to recycle baking sheets.

Bake biscuits 10–12 minutes, or until top of biscuit feels slightly firm when touched with fingertip; do not overbake or biscuits will be dry. Transfer to wire rack for 2–3 minutes, just until set. With a palette knife, transfer biscuits to wire rack to cool completely.

SWEET SUCCESS

These biscuits are best eaten as fresh as possible as they dry slightly on storage, but they will last for several days in an airtight container. Pack them in single layers so the tops are not damaged.

CHOCOLATE AND HAZELNUT PINWHEELS

MAKES ABOUT 60

This two-toned biscuit is unusually flavourful. The combination of the light orange-flavoured dough and the mocha and hazelnut flavoured chocolate works well.

25 g/1 oz hazelnuts
45 ml/3 tbsp cocoa powder
225 g/8 oz unsalted butter, softened
175 g/6 oz sugar
1 egg
5 ml/1 tsp vanilla essence
finely grated zest of 1 orange or
   2.5 ml/½ tsp orange essence
2.5 ml/½ tsp coffee powder, dissolved
   in 7.5 ml/1½ tsp water

Preheat oven to 180°C/350°F/Gas Mark 4. Place hazelnuts on a small baking sheet and toast 12–15 minutes, until golden brown, turning nuts once. Turn off oven. Cool nuts slightly. To remove skins, rub the hazelnuts in a clean dish-towel or place in a sieve and rub together. Toss in a coarse sieve to remove the skins.

Place hazelnuts in a food processor fitted with the metal blade and process until coarsely chopped. Add cocoa powder and using *pulse action*, process until nuts are very finely chopped but not oily. Set aside.

With electric mixer, beat butter and sugar 2–3 minutes, until light and creamy. Add the egg, vanilla and orange zest and continue beating until well blended and smooth.

Gradually stir in flour and salt, just until blended. Line work surface with large sheet of waxed paper and transfer half the plain biscuit dough to waxed paper. Cover with another sheet of waxed paper and roll out dough to a 20 × 27.5 cm/8 × 11 in rectangle. Slide onto a large baking sheet or tray and refrigerate while preparing remaining chocolate dough.

Beat hazelnut and cocoa mixture and dissolved coffee powder into plain dough remaining in bowl, just until well blended and smooth. Place a large sheet of waxed paper on work surface and scrape dough onto paper. Cover with another sheet of waxed paper and roll out to a 20 × 27.5 cm/8 × 11 in rect-angle.

Remove waxed paper from tops of chocolate and plain doughs. Invert chocolate dough onto plain dough pressing together gently and chill, covered, until slightly firm but flexible, about 15 minutes.

Slide dough onto work surface and remove waxed paper from layers. Trim edges straight. Using waxed paper under the plain dough as a guide and starting from a long edge, roll dough tightly, swiss-roll fashion. Wrap log in waxed paper and freeze at least 1 hour or until firm.

Preheat oven to 180°C/350°F/Gas Mark 4. Grease 2 or more baking sheets. Using a large sharp knife, cut frozen log into 3 mm/⅛ in slices and place on baking sheets about 2.5 cm/1 in apart. Bake 5–8 minutes, or until biscuits are golden at the edges.

Transfer to wire rack 2–3 minutes, until set. Using palette knife, transfer biscuits to wire rack to cool completely. Biscuits will keep in an airtight container for 1 week.

SWEET SUCCESS

This is a refrigerator biscuit which can be prepared ahead and baked as required.

WHITE CHOCOLATE FRUIT N' NUT BARS

MAKES ABOUT 20

This bar biscuit is jam packed with fruit and nuts. It's sweet and chewy and easy to make and keep – ideal for children's lunchboxes.

65 g/2½ oz slivered almonds, toasted
100 g/4 oz brazil or hazelnuts, coarsely
    chopped
100 g/4 oz chopped dried apricots
150 g/5 oz raisins
150 g/5 oz chopped dates
65 g/2½ oz shredded coconut
40 g/1½ oz plain flour
225 g/8 oz good quality white
    chocolate, chopped
120 ml/4 fl oz double cream
120 ml/4 fl oz apricot jam
120 ml/4 fl oz honey
15 g/1 oz good quality white chocolate,
    melted, for decoration

Preheat oven to 170°C/325°F/Gas Mark 3. Grease 20 × 30 cm/8 × 12 in baking tin. Line bottom with non-stick parchment paper or foil and grease paper or foil.

In a bowl, combine almonds, brazils, apricots, raisins, dates, coconut and flour.

In a saucepan over low heat, melt chocolate and cream, stirring frequently until smooth. Stir in apricot jam and honey until well blended. Stir white chocolate mixture into fruit and nut mixture and scrape into prepared tin. Spread mixture evenly, smoothing top.

Bake 30–35 minutes, until set. Transfer to wire rack to cool in tin. Invert onto baking sheet and remove paper, invert back onto wire rack topside up. Drizzle with white chocolate and cut into bars.

BLACK-AND-WHITE CHOCOLATE-MINT SANDWICH BISCUITS

MAKES ABOUT 20

This is a very upmarket version of a chocolate sandwich biscuit. A filling of rich, white chocolate ganache is sandwiched between chocolate cookies; then glazed with dark chocolate.

100 g/4 oz unsalted butter, softened
50 g/2 oz sugar
1 egg
5 ml/1 tsp peppermint essence
25 g/1 oz cocoa powder
100 g/4 oz plain flour

WHITE CHOCOLATE GANACHE FILLING

120 ml/4 fl oz whipping cream
175 g/6 oz good quality white chocolate, chopped
5 ml/1 tsp peppermint essence

150 g/5 oz plain chocolate, chopped
40 g/1½ oz unsalted butter

With electric mixer, beat butter and sugar until light and creamy, about 3 minutes. Add egg and beat 2–3 minutes longer, until mixture is fluffy. Beat in peppermint essence.

Into a bowl, sift cocoa and flour together. With a wooden spoon, gradually stir into the creamy butter mixture just until blended. Turn out dough onto a piece of plastic wrap and use to flatten dough to a thick disc. Wrap and refrigerate at least 1 hour, or until cold.

Preheat oven to 180°C/350°F/Gas Mark 4. Grease and flour 2 large baking sheets. Remove dough from the refrigerator and divide in half. Refrigerate one half of dough.

On a lightly floured surface, roll out the other half of dough to about 3 mm/⅛ in thick. Using a floured heart-shaped or flower-shaped cutter, about 5 cm/2 in in diameter, cut out as many shapes as possible and place the shapes on pre-

pared baking sheets; reserve any trimmings. Repeat with second half of dough. Gather up trimmings, roll out as above and cut out as many additional shapes as possible; be sure to have an equal number of shapes.

Bake 7–8 minutes, until edges are set; do not overbake as biscuits burn easily. Transfer to wire racks to cool 10 minutes. With a palette knife, transfer biscuits to wire rack to cool completely.

Prepare filling. In a saucepan over medium heat, bring cream to the boil. Remove from heat. Add white chocolate all at once, stirring constantly until smooth. Stir in peppermint essence and pour into bowl. Cool about 1 hour until firm but not hard.

With hand-held electric mixer, beat white chocolate filling 30–45 seconds, until it becomes lighter and fluffier. Spread a little white chocolate filling onto bottom side of 1 biscuit and imme-

diately cover it with another biscuit, pressing together gently. Repeat with remaining biscuits and filling. Refrigerate 30 minutes, or until firm.

In a saucepan over low heat, melt chocolate and butter, stirring frequently until smooth. Remove from heat. Cool 15 minutes until slightly thickened.

Spread a small amount of glaze onto the top of each sandwiched biscuit, being careful not to let glaze drip or spread over edges. Chill until glaze is set.

CHUNKY CHOCOLATE BROWNIES WITH FUDGE GLAZE

MAKES 14–16 SERVINGS

A very moist, fudgy brownie filled with chopped pecans and chunks of white chocolate.

275 g/10 oz bittersweet chocolate, chopped
50 g/2 oz unsalted butter, cut into pieces
75 g/3 oz brown sugar
50 g/2 oz granulated sugar
2 eggs
15 ml/1 tbsp vanilla essence
50 g/2 oz plain flour
90 g/3½ oz pecans or walnuts, chopped and toasted
150 g/5 oz good quality white chocolate, chopped into 0.5 cm/¼ in pieces

FUDGY CHOCOLATE GLAZE
175 g/6 oz plain chocolate, chopped
50 g/2 oz unsalted butter, cut into pieces
30 ml/2 tbsp golden syrup
10 ml/2 tsp vanilla essence
5 ml/1 tsp instant coffee powder

Preheat oven to 180°C/350°F/Gas Mark 4. Invert a 20 cm/8 in square baking tin and mould a piece of foil over bottom. Turn tin over and line with moulded foil. Lightly grease foil.

In a saucepan over low heat, melt chocolates and butter, stirring frequently until smooth. Remove pan from heat.

Stir in sugars and continue stirring 2 minutes longer, until sugar is dissolved. Beat in eggs and vanilla. Stir in flour until blended. Stir in pecans and chopped chocolate. Pour into pan.

Bake 20–25 minutes, until a cocktail stick or fine skewer inserted 5 cm/2 in from centre comes out with just a few crumbs attached; do not overbake. Transfer to wire rack to cool 30 minutes. Using foil as a guide, remove brownie from tin and cool on rack at least 2 hours.

Prepare glaze. In a saucepan over medium heat, melt the chocolate, butter, golden syrup, vanilla and coffee powder, stirring frequently until smooth. Remove from heat. Refrigerate 1 hour, or until thickened and spreadable.

Invert brownie onto plate and remove foil. Invert back onto rack and slide onto serving plate, top-side up. Using palette knife, spread a thick layer of glaze over top of brownie just to edges. Refrigerate 1 hour, until set. Cut into squares or bars.

CHUNKY CHOCOLATE BROWNIES WITH FUDGE GLAZE ▶

CHOCOLATE AND PECAN MERINGUES

MAKES 22–24

These meringues are hard to describe – somewhere between a biscuit and a sweet biscuit, they were always amongst the Christmas biscuits made by my mother's best friend, a real American Southern belle and a marvellous baker.

4 egg whites
1.5 ml/¼ tsp cream of tartar
225 g/8 oz sugar
10 ml/2 tsp vanilla essence
90 g/3½ oz pecans, chopped and toasted
175 g/6 oz chocolate chips

Preheat oven to 110°C/225°F/Gas Mark ¼. Line 2 large baking sheets with foil, shiny side up.

With electric mixer, beat whites and cream of tartar until soft peaks form. Continue beating and begin adding sugar, 15 ml/1 tbsp at a time, beating at least 1 minute after each addition; this takes about 15 minutes. Continue beating 4–5 more minutes, until whites are very stiff and glossy and sugar is completely dissolved. Beat in vanilla essence. Fold in nuts and chocolate.

Use a tablespoon to scoop up a mounded ball of meringue for each biscuit, then use another tablespoon to scrape off onto baking sheets. Make each meringue with tall, rough peaks to look really spectacular.

Bake 2 hours, turning baking sheets and reversing top sheet with bottom sheet to ensure even baking. Turn off heat, but leave meringue to dry for 1 hour longer, until completely dry. They should not colour too much. Remove meringues from oven and peel each off foil. Meringues can be stored in airtight containers.

CHOCOLATE AND COCONUT SARAH BERNHARDTS

These delicious, chewy, chocolate biscuits are probably called Sarah Bernhardts because they too go over-the-top — except with chocolate! Chocolate-dipped, ganache-topped, chocolate macaroons — there's no more room for any more chocolate.

90 g/3½ oz shredded coconut
75 g/3 oz sugar
30 ml/2 tbsp plain flour
45 ml/3 tbsp cocoa powder
5 ml/1 tsp vanilla essence
15 ml/1 tbsp golden syrup
2–3 egg whites

GANACHE TOPPING
175 ml/6 fl oz cream
225 g/8 oz plain chocolate, chopped
25 g/1 oz unsalted butter, cut into pieces
30 ml/2 tbsp shredded coconut

CHOCOLATE GLAZE
175 g/6 oz plain chocolate, chopped
25 g/1 oz unsalted butter, cut into pieces
15 ml/1 tbsp golden syrup

Prepare topping. In a medium saucepan over medium heat, bring cream to the boil. Remove from heat. Add chocolate all at once, stirring well until melted and smooth. Beat in butter. Cool, then refrigerate 1–2 hours, until thickened and chilled, but not set.

Preheat oven to 170°C/325°F/Gas Mark 3. Line a large baking sheet with foil; grease foil. In a bowl, combine coconut, sugar, flour and cocoa powder. Stir in the vanilla and golden syrup and 2 egg whites; if mixture is too dry, add the third egg white, little by little, until a thick dough-like batter forms and holds together.

Using a miniature ice cream scoop, about 2.5 cm/1 in in diameter, or a teaspoon, place 16 scoops onto baking sheet. With index finger, flatten each scoop, making a slight indentation in centre of each.

Bake 12–14 minutes, just until cookies are set on the outside. Do not overbake or the macaroons will be too hard. Cool on baking sheet 10–15 minutes, then remove from foil to wire rack to cool completely.

When topping mixture is cold and thick, beat with an electric mixer 30–45 seconds, just until mixture lightens in colour and thickens enough to pipe; do not overbeat or mixture will become grainy.

Quickly spoon mixture into a large piping bag fitted with a 1 cm/½ in plain nozzle and pipe a 2.5 cm/1 in mound on top of each macaroon, pressing tip firmly onto centre of each biscuit. Chill 1–2 hours, until topping is firm.

Prepare glaze. In a small saucepan over low heat, melt chocolate and butter with golden syrup, stirring frequently until smooth. Pour into tall, narrow container, mug or strong paper cup to allow easier dipping. Cool chocolate.

Holding each macaroon by the very bottom edge, carefully and quickly dip each biscuit into chocolate glaze to cover filling and top of each macaroon to within about 0.5 cm/¼ in of bottom, twisting and swirling in chocolate glaze so entire biscuit is coated. Leave excess to drip off, then quickly turn upright and place on baking sheet. Decorate the tops with a sprinkling of coconut.

COCOA BROWNIES WITH MILK CHOCOLATE AND WALNUT TOPPING

12 SERVINGS

This brownie is moist and dense but less fudgy because it uses cocoa instead of chocolate, but still has a dark, brownie-like texture. The milk chocolate and walnut topping is quick and easy to make.

50 g/2 oz plain flour
40 g/1½ oz cocoa powder
1.5 ml/¼ tsp baking powder
1.5 ml/¼ tsp salt
100 g/4 oz unsalted butter
225 g/8 oz sugar
2 eggs
10 ml/2 tsp vanilla essence
75 g/3 oz walnuts, coarsely chopped

MILK CHOCOLATE AND WALNUT TOPPING
175–200 g/6–7 oz milk chocolate
75 g/3 oz walnuts, chopped

Preheat oven to 180°C/350°F/Gas Mark 4. Grease a 23 cm/9 in springform tin or 23 cm/9 in cake tin with removable bottom. Into a bowl, sift flour, cocoa powder, baking powder and salt. Set aside.

In medium saucepan over medium heat, melt butter. Stir in sugar and remove from the heat, stirring 2 to 3 minutes to dissolve sugar. Beat in eggs and vanilla. Stir in the flour mixture just until blended; then stir in walnuts. Pour into the prepared tin, smoothing top evenly.

Bake 18–24 minutes, until a cocktail stick or fine skewer inserted 5 cm/2 in from the centre comes out with just a few crumbs attached; do not overbake or brownie will be dry.

Prepare topping. Break milk chocolate into pieces. As soon as brownie tests done, remove from the oven to a heat-proof surface. Quickly place chocolate pieces all over the top of the brownies; do not let chocolate touch side of tin. Return to the oven 20–30 seconds.

Remove brownie and, with the back of a spoon, gently spread softened chocolate evenly over the top. Sprinkle walnuts evenly over the top and, with the back of a spoon, gently press them into chocolate. Cool on wire rack 30 minutes.

Refrigerate 1 hour, until set. Run a knife around edge of tin to loosen brownie from edge. Carefully remove side of tin. Cool completely and serve at room temperature.

CREAM CHEESE-MARBLED BROWNIES

15–20 SERVINGS

This is the best of two worlds: a moist, dense brownie marbled with a cream cheese layer – brownie and cheesecake. The contrast in colour as well as flavour makes this a great chocolate combination.

250 g/9 oz bittersweet chocolate, chopped
225 g/8 oz unsalted butter, softened
150 g/5 oz sugar
50 g/2 oz soft brown sugar
3 eggs
15 ml/1 tbsp vanilla essence
100 g/4 oz plain flour
1.5 ml/¼ tsp salt
450 g/1 lb cream cheese, softened
75 g/3 oz sugar
1 egg
5 ml/1 tsp vanilla essence
finely grated zest of 1 lemon

Preheat oven to 180°C/350°F/Gas Mark 4. Invert a 23 × 32.5 cm/9 × 13 in baking tin and mould foil over bottom. Turn tin over and line with foil; leave foil to extend above sides of tin. Grease bottom and sides of foil.

In a saucepan over low heat, melt chocolate and 100 g//4 oz butter, stirring frequently until smooth. Remove from heat. Cool to room temperature.

In a bowl using hand-held mixer, beat remaining butter, the 150 g/5 oz sugar and the brown sugar until light and creamy, 2–3 minutes. Add eggs, 1 at a time, beating well after each addition. Beat in vanilla, then slowly beat in melted chocolate and butter. Stir in the flour and salt just until blended.

In a bowl using hand-held electric mixer, beat cream cheese and 75 g/3 oz sugar until smooth, about 1 minute. Beat in egg, vanilla and lemon zest.

Pour two-thirds of the brownie batter into tin and spread evenly. Pour cream cheese mixture over the brownie layer. Spoon remaining one-third brownie mixture in dollops on top of cream cheese mixture in 2 rows along long side of tin. Using a knife or spoon, swirl brownie batter into the cream cheese batter to create marble effect.

Bake 25–35 minutes, or until a cocktail stick or fine skewer inserted 5 cm/ 2 in from edge of tin comes out with just a few crumbs attached. Transfer to wire rack to cool in tin.

When cool, use foil to help lift brownie out of tin. Invert onto another rack or baking sheet and peel off foil. Invert back onto wire rack and slide onto serving plate. Cut into squares and wrap and refrigerate; or wrap until ready to serve, then cut into squares.

Sweets

EASY CHOCOLATE TRUFFLES

CHOCOLATE-COATED RASPBERRY TRUFFLES

MILK CHOCOLATE AND PISTACHIO COATED TRUFFLES

CHOCOLATE-FILLED FIGS AND PRUNES

WHITE CHOCOLATE FUDGE LAYER

CHOCOLATE MINT CRISPS

CHOCOLATE-COATED TOFFEE

CHOCOLATE FONDUE

CHOCOLATE 'TURTLES'

DOUBLE CHOCOLATE-DIPPED FRUIT

CHOCOLATE-DIPPED CARAMEL APPLES

EASY CHOCOLATE TRUFFLES

Most chocolate truffles are made from a chocolate ganache base—chocolate and cream or butter, often with the addition of brandy or liqueur as a flavouring. The easiest and most authentic truffles are those irregularly shaped and rolled in cocoa to resemble the real truffle. Truffles can be dipped in chocolate or nuts and the combinations are almost endless; these are easy and foolproof.

150 ml/5 fl oz whipping cream
250 g/9 oz plain chocolate, chopped
30 ml/2 tbsp brandy or other liqueur
  (optional)
cocoa powder for dusting

In a saucepan over low heat, bring cream to the boil. Remove pan from heat. Add chocolate all at once, stirring frequently until smooth. Stir in liqueur if using. Strain into a bowl and cool to room temperature. Refrigerate 1 hour, until thickened and firm.

Line 2 small baking sheets with foil. Using a melon baller, a 2.5 cm/1 in ice cream scoop or teaspoon, form mixture into 2.5 cm/1 in balls and place on baking sheets. Refrigerate 1–2 hours, until balls are firm.

Place about 50 g/2 oz cocoa powder in a small bowl. Drop each chocolate ball into cocoa and turn with fingers to coat with cocoa. Roll balls between the palms of your hands, dusting with more cocoa if necessary. Do not try to make them perfectly round; they should look slightly irregular. Place on baking sheet. Add more cocoa to bowl if necessary.

Shake cocoa-coated truffles in a dry sieve to remove excess cocoa, then store, covered, in the refrigerator up to 2 weeks or freeze up to 2 months. Soften 10 minutes at room temperature before serving.

CHOCOLATE-COATED RASPBERRY TRUFFLES

The combination of chocolate and raspberry is perfection and these truffles are a great example of a perfect marriage. They are coated in crisp, dark chocolate, but could be rolled in cocoa powder as in Easy Chocolate Truffles.

275 g/10 oz bittersweet chocolate, chopped
75 g/3 oz unsalted butter, cut into pieces
75 ml/2½ fl oz seedless raspberry jam
30 ml/2 tbsp raspberry-flavoured liqueur
350 g/12 oz chocolate, chopped (for coating)

In a saucepan over low heat, melt the 275 g/10 oz chocolate, butter and jam, stirring frequently until smooth and well blended. Remove from heat and stir in liqueur. Strain into a bowl and cool. Refrigerate 2–3 hours, until firm.

Line a baking sheet with waxed paper or foil. Using a melon baller, a 2.5 cm/1 in ice cream scoop or teaspoon, form mixture into balls. Place on baking sheet and freeze 1 hour, or until very firm.

In the top of a double boiler over low heat, melt remaining chocolate, stirring frequently until smooth; chocolate should be 46–48°C/115°–120°F. Remove from heat and pour into a clean bowl; cool to about 30°C/88°F.

Using a fork, dip truffles, 1 at a time, into chocolate, coating completely and tapping fork on edge of bowl to shake off excess. Place on prepared baking sheet. Refrigerate until chocolate is set, about 1 hour. Store in an airtight container with paper towels covering truffles to collect any moisture up to 2 weeks or 1 month in freezer.

For white chocolate coating, melt 450 g/1 lb white chocolate as directed, but cool to about 29°C/84°F before coating truffles. Top each truffle with a candied rose petal or violet. Refrigerate as directed.

MILK CHOCOLATE AND PISTACHIO COATED TRUFFLES

MAKES ABOUT 24

This truffle is for lovers of milk chocolate. The mild, creamy centre is coated with dark chocolate, then quickly dipped into chopped pistachios.

120 ml/4 fl oz double or whipping cream

350 g/12 oz good quality milk chocolate, chopped

15 g/½ oz unsalted butter

15 ml/1 tbsp almond or hazelnut flavoured-liqueur

350 g/12 oz bittersweet chocolate, chopped

150 g/5 oz shelled and unsalted pistachio nuts, finely chopped

In a medium saucepan over medium heat, bring cream to the boil. Remove from heat. Add chocolate all at once, stirring until melted. Stir in butter and liqueur. Strain into bowl. Refrigerate 1 hour or until firm.

Line a baking sheet with waxed paper or foil. Using a melon baller, a 2.5 cm/ 1 in ice cream scoop or teaspoon, form mixture into balls. Place on baking sheet and freeze 1 hour, or until very firm.

In the top of a double boiler over low heat, melt chocolate, stirring frequently until smooth; chocolate should be about 46–48°C/115°–120°F. Remove from heat and pour into a clean bowl; cool to about 30°C/88°F.

Place pistachios in a bowl. Using a fork, dip truffles, 1 at a time, into chocolate, coating completely and tapping fork on edge of bowl to shake off excess. Immediately drop into bowl of pistachios and roll to coat chocolate completely. Place on prepared baking sheet. Refrigerate until set, about 1 hour. Store in an airtight container with paper towels covering truffles to collect any moisture up to 2 weeks or 1 month in the freezer.

SWEET SUCCESS

Truffles can be coated with chocolate only, then drizzled with white or milk chocolate or simply rolled in nuts without chocolate coating.

CHOCOLATE-STUFFED FIGS AND PRUNES

MAKES 24

These little sweetmeats are easy to make and look very pretty if served in little gold sweet cases. If figs are unavailable dates would do just as well.

12 large fresh figs
12 extra-large prunes, preferably
    presoaked or softened
40 g/1½ oz unsalted butter, softened
75 g/3 oz blanched almonds, chopped
    and toasted
1 egg yolk
15 ml/1 tbsp Amaretto liqueur
75 g/3 oz plain chocolate, melted and
    cooled

CHOCOLATE FOR DIPPING
225 g/8 oz plain chocolate, chopped
65 g/2½ oz unsalted butter, cut into
    pieces

Using a small knife, remove any remains of the stem of the figs. If necessary, stone prunes the same way. Set aside.

Into a food processor fitted with the metal blade, process butter, almonds, egg yolk and liqueur until creamy. With the machine running, slowly pour in the melted chocolate and process until well blended. Scrape into a bowl and refrigerate about 1 hour, until firm enough to pipe.

Line a baking sheet with waxed paper. Spoon mixture into small piping bag fitted with a small plain nozzle, about 0.5 cm/¼ in. Pipe mixture into figs and prunes. Place filled fruits on baking sheet and chill 30 minutes.

In a saucepan over low heat, melt chocolate and butter, stirring frequently until melted and smooth. Leave to cool to room temperature, about 30 minutes, stirring occasionally.

Insert a cocktail stick into each filled fruit. Dip each into the melted chocolate and allow excess to drip off. Using another cocktail stick, push fruit off the inserted cocktail stick onto the lined baking sheet. Alternatively, holding stem end, dip filled fruits about two-thirds of the way into the chocolate, leaving one-third of the fruit exposed. Place on baking sheet. Refrigerate at least 1 hour to set.

Using a thin-bladed knife, remove fruit from baking sheet to paper cases. Remove from refrigerator about 30 minutes before serving.

SWEET SUCCESS

If you prefer, slice filled figs and prunes crosswise, exposing the filling and arrange on a small serving plate.

SWEETS

WHITE CHOCOLATE FUDGE LAYER

MAKES 36 TRIANGLES

This creamy, white chocolate fudge has a layer of dark chocolate in the middle. It is important to chill each layer before the next if you want a distinct line.

600 g/1¼ lbs good quality white chocolate, chopped
400 g/14 oz can sweetened condensed milk
10 ml/2 tsp vanilla essence
7.5 ml/1½ tsp white vinegar or lemon juice
pinch salt
250 g/9 oz unsalted macadamia nuts
175 g/6 oz plain chocolate, chopped
40 g/1½ oz unsalted butter, cut into pieces
25 g/1 oz plain chocolate, melted, for piping

Line a 20 cm/8 in square cake tin with foil. Invert tin. Mould foil over bottom, then turn cake tin right side up and line with foil. Grease bottom and sides of foil. Set aside.

In a saucepan over low heat, melt chocolate with condensed milk, stirring frequently until smooth. Remove from heat and stir in vanilla, vinegar and salt until well blended. Stir in nuts. Spread half of white chocolate mixture in tin. Refrigerate 15 minutes or until firm; keep remaining mixture warm.

In a saucepan over low heat, melt 175 g/6 oz plain chocolate and butter, stirring frequently until smooth. Cool slightly; pour over white chocolate layer and refrigerate until firm, about 15 minutes.

If necessary, gently reheat white chocolate mixture and pour over set chocolate layer, smoothing top evenly. Refrigerate 2–4 hours, until completely firm.

Using foil as a guide, remove set fudge from tin. With knife, cut into 16 squares. Cut each square diagonally in half, making 36 triangles. Place fudge triangles onto wire rack placed over a baking sheet to catch drips.

Spoon melted chocolate into small paper cone (see Decorating with Chocolate) and drizzle chocolate over fudge triangles. Store in an airtight container in refrigerator 1–2 weeks.

CHOCOLATE MINT CRISPS

These after-dinner mints are easy to make, and are an ideal hostess gift. Try replacing the mint with orange for a change.

vegetable oil for greasing
60 ml/4 tbsp sugar
60 ml/2 fl oz water
5 ml/1 tsp peppermint essence
225 g/8 oz plain chocolate, chopped

Grease a baking sheet with vegetable oil. Set aside. In a saucepan, bring sugar and water to the boil, swirling pan until sugar dissolves. Boil rapidly until sugar reaches 140°C/280°F on a sugar thermometer (see "Sweet Success"). Remove pan from heat and stir in peppermint essence. Pour onto greased baking sheet and allow to set; do not touch as the sugar syrup is very hot and can cause serious burns.

When mixture is cold, use a rolling pin to break up into pieces. Place pieces into a food processor fitted with the metal blade and process until fine crumbs form; do not overprocess.

Line 2 baking sheets with waxed paper or foil; grease paper or foil. In the top of a double boiler over low heat, melt chocolate, stirring frequently until smooth. Remove from heat and stir in ground mint mixture.

Using a teaspoon, drop small mounds of mixture onto prepared baking sheets. Using the back of the spoon, spread into 2.5 cm/1 in circles. Cool, then refrigerate to set, at least 1 hour. Peel off paper and store in airtight containers with waxed paper between each layer. Store in the refrigerator for 1 week.

SWEET SUCCESS

If you do not have a sugar thermometer, test the temperature of the boiling sugar by pouring a few drops of syrup into a small bowl of cold water; it should become brittle and snap within 1 minute. Do not touch the brittle sugar until it cools in the water for several seconds.

CHOCOLATE-COATED TOFFEE

MAKES ABOUT 750 G

This is a very buttery toffee coated with a thick layer of chocolate, then sprinkled with chopped pecans. Break the pieces into irregular shapes and wrap in cellophane for an attractive gift.

150 g/5 oz pecans (optional)
225 g/8 oz unsalted butter, cut into
  pieces
350 g/12 oz sugar
1.5 ml/¼ tsp cream of tartar
175 g/6 oz plain chocolate, finely
  chopped

Preheat oven to 180°C/350°F/Gas Mark 4. Place pecans (if using) on a small baking sheet and bake 10–12 minutes, until well toasted. Leave to cool completely, then chop and set aside.

Line a 23 cm/9 in square cake tin with foil. Invert tin and mould foil over bottom. Turn tin right side up and line with moulded foil. Generously butter bottom and sides of foil.

In a heavy-bottomed saucepan over medium heat, melt butter. Stir in sugar and cream of tartar, stirring until sugar dissolves. Bring mixture to the boil. Cover tin for 2 minutes so steam washes down any sugar crystals which collect on side of tin. Uncover and continue cooking 10–12 minutes, or until toffee reaches 310°F on a sweet thermometer.

Carefully pour into tin and leave to rest about 1 minute. Sprinkle top of toffee with chocolate and leave 2 minutes until chocolate softens. Using the back of a spoon or a wide-bladed knife, spread chocolate evenly over toffee until smooth. Sprinkle evenly with the chopped pecans (if using). Cool to room temperature, then refrigerate until firm and cold.

Using foil as a guide, remove toffee from tin. With the back of a heavy knife or hammer, break toffee into large, irregular pieces. Store in an airtight container for about a week in the refrigerator.

CHOCOLATE COATED TOFFEE ▶

CHOCOLATE FONDUE

8 SERVINGS

This is an ideal dessert for real chocolate lovers; the dipping pieces are just a vehicle for tasting the pure flavour of thick, melted chocolate — use the best.

fresh strawberries; seedless grapes;
sliced bananas (sprinkled with a little
lemon juice); peeled orange segments;
fresh pineapple chunks; fresh cherries;
cubes of sponge cake or angel-food
cake; marshmallows
250 ml/8 fl oz double or whipping
  cream
450 g/1 lb plain chocolate, chopped
30 ml/2 tbsp brandy or other liqueur

Prepare ingredients for dipping. Wipe or wash fresh fruits and dry well; place on paper towel to absorb any moisture. Cube pieces of cake.

In a saucepan over medium heat, bring cream to the boil. Remove from heat and add the chocolate all at once, stirring until smooth. Stir in liqueur. Transfer to a fondue pot and keep warm.

Arrange fruit and cake pieces attractively on a large serving platter. Furnish each guest with a fondue fork and allow each guest to dip pieces of fruit, cake and marshmallows into warm chocolate.

VARIATION

For a white chocolate fondue, prepare as above but use 150 ml/5 fl oz double cream, 350 g/12 oz good quality white chocolate, chopped, and 15–30 ml/ 1–2 tbsp liqueur. Dip in any variety of fruits and substitute chocolate cake or brownie cubes for sponge or angel cake.

CHOCOLATE "TURTLES"

These chocolate-covered nut clusters are an all-time favourite. Use the nuts you like most or a combination, but be sure they are all about the same size.

vegetable oil
Caramel Coating (p106)
275 g/10 oz hazelnuts, pecans, walnuts or unsalted peanuts or a combination
350 g/12 oz plain chocolate, chopped
30 ml/2 tbsp white vegetable fat

Oil 2 baking sheets with the vegetable oil. Prepare the caramel coating.

When caramel has cooled a few minutes, stir in nuts until they are coated. Using an oiled tablespoon, drop spoonsful of caramel-nut mixture onto prepared baking sheet, about 2.5 cm/ 1 in apart. If caramel-nut mixture becomes too hard, reheat over low heat several minutes until softened. Refrigerate until firm and cold.

Using a palette knife, transfer nut clusters to a wire rack over a baking sheet to catch drips. In a saucepan over low heat, melt chocolate and vegetable fat, stirring occasionally until smooth; cool chocolate to about 30°C/88°F.

Using a tablespoon, spoon chocolate over nut clusters, being sure to coat completely, spreading chocolate over surface. Return drips to saucepan and reheat gently to completely cover all clusters. Leave to set about 2 hours at room temperature. Store in a cool place in an airtight container with foil between layers, but do not refrigerate.

When stirring nuts into caramel, stir just until coated. Do not overwork or caramel will crystallize.

DOUBLE CHOCOLATE-DIPPED FRUIT

MAKES ABOUT 12

Just about any kind of fruit can be dipped in chocolate as long as it is dry-dry-dry; even a drop of moisture can cause the melted chocolate to seize and harden. To store chocolate-dipped fruits more than 12 hours, the chocolate should be tempered (see p8). For serving the same day, pure melted chocolate can be used.

about 12 pieces of fruit, such as strawberries; cherries; orange segments; kiwi fruit; fresh peeled lychees; Cape gooseberries; stoned prunes; stoned dates; dried apricots; dried pears; nuts
175 g/6 oz quality white chocolate, chopped
75 g/3 oz plain chocolate, chopped

Clean and prepare fruits. Wipe strawberries with a soft cloth or brush gently with pastry brush; wash and dry firm skinned fruits such as cherries and grapes. Dry well and set on paper towels to absorb any remaining moisture. Peel or cut any other fruits being used. Dried or candied fruits can also be used.

In the top of a double boiler over low heat, melt white chocolate, stirring frequently until smooth. Remove from heat and cool to tepid, about 84°F, stirring frequently.

Line baking sheet with waxed paper or foil. Holding fruits by the stem or end and at an angle, dip about two thirds of the fruit into the chocolate. Allow excess to drip off and place on baking sheet. Continue dipping fruits; if chocolate becomes too thick, set over hot water again briefly to soften slightly. Refrigerate fruits until chocolate sets, about 20 minutes.

In the top of the cleaned double boiler over low heat, melt plain chocolate, stirring frequently until smooth. Remove from heat and cool to just below body temperature, about 30°C/88°F.

Remove each white chocolate-coated fruit from baking sheet and holding each by the stem or end, and at the opposite angle, dip bottom third of each piece into the dark chocolate, creating a chevron effect. Set on baking sheet. Refrigerate 15 minutes, or until set. Remove from refrigerator 10–15 minutes before serving to soften chocolate.

SWEET SUCCESS

If the chocolate is carefully melted and cooled and the fruits kept refrigerated, the chocolate should remain glossy for several hours. This is sufficient for fresh soft fruits such as strawberries and grapes. If you wish to store dipped dried or candied fruits for a longer period, it is better to temper the chocolate, which allows the fruits to be stored several weeks at room temperature (see Cooking with Chocolate).

SWEETS

CHOCOLATE-DIPPED CARAMEL APPLES

MAKES 12

This old-fashioned Halloween treat takes on a new dimension when coated with rich, dark chocolate. Choose small apples so there is plenty of chocolate and caramel to apple.

vegetable oil
12 small apples, well scrubbed and
    dried
90 g/3½ oz pecans, walnuts or
    hazelnuts, finely chopped and toasted
    (optional)
175 g/6 oz chocolate, chopped

CARAMEL COATING
520 ml/18 fl oz double cream
350 ml/12 fl oz golden syrup
40 g/1½ oz unsalted butter, cut into
    pieces
225 g/8 oz granulated sugar
90 g/3½ oz brown sugar
pinch salt
15 ml/1 tbsp vanilla essence

Oil a baking sheet with the vegetable oil. Insert a wooden lollipop stick firmly into the stem end of each apple; do not use metal sticks or small pointed wooden skewers as they could be harmful to children.

In a heavy-bottomed saucepan, stir cream, syrup, butter, sugars and salt. Cook over medium heat, stirring occasionally until sugars dissolve and butter is melted, about 3 minutes. Bring mixture to the boil and cook, stirring frequently, until caramel mixture reaches 240°F (soft-ball stage) on a sugar thermometer (see "Sweet Success"), about 20 minutes. Place bottom of saucepan in a pan of cold water to stop cooking or transfer to a small, cold saucepan. Cool to about 104°C/220°F; this will take 10–15 minutes. Stir in vanilla.

Holding each apple by wooden stick, quickly dip each apple into hot caramel, turning to coat on all sides and covering apple completely. Scrape bottom of apple against edge of saucepan to remove excess; place on prepared baking sheet. If necessary, reheat caramel slightly to thin slightly. Leave apples to cool 15–20 minutes, until caramel hardens.

If using, place nuts in a bowl. In the top of a double boiler over low heat, melt chocolate, stirring frequently until smooth. Remove from heat. Dip each caramel-coated apple about two-thirds way into chocolate, allowing excess to drip off, then dip into nuts. Return to waxed paper-lined baking sheet. Leave to set 1 hour, until chocolate hardens.

Drinks

CONTINENTAL HOT CHOCOLATE

SPICY HOT COCOA

VELVETY HOT CHOCOLATE

RICH ICED CHOCOLATE

EXTRA-CHOCOLATE MILK SHAKE

CHOCOLATE CREAM LIQUEUR

DELUXE CHOCOLATE EGG NOG

CONTINENTAL HOT CHOCOLATE

MAKES 1 CUP

This is the kind of hot chocolate that was served in the early chocolate houses of Europe. It is a bitter-sweet drink that can be substituted for a strong, after-dinner coffee.

40 g/1½ oz plain chocolate, chopped
7.5 ml/1½ tsp cocoa powder
pinch salt
2.5 ml/½ tsp sugar
milk

Place chocolate, cocoa powder, salt and sugar in a small saucepan. Using the cup in which the chocolate will be served, fill it about one-quarter full of milk and then add enough water to almost fill cup.

Add the milk and water to the saucepan and, over medium heat, bring to a boil, beating constantly until chocolate is melted and smooth. Boil for 30 seconds longer, beating until foamy, then pour into cup. Serve immediately.

SWEET SUCCESS

Heat the cup by pouring some hot water in it while making the chocolate. Empty and dry the cup before filling with hot chocolate.

FROM TOP RIGHT, CLOCKWISE: CONTINENTAL HOT CHOCOLATE, SPICY HOT COCOA, AND VELVETY HOT CHOCOLATE ▶

SPICY HOT COCOA

4 SERVINGS

Hot cocoa is the traditional chocolate drink that always satisfies. It was always waiting for us after sleigh-riding or ice skating, and the smell always brings back childhood memories. I've added some extra spice to this one.

75 g/3 oz sugar
40 g/1½ oz cocoa powder
2.5 ml/½ tsp grated nutmeg
2.5 ml/½ tsp ground cloves
2.5 ml/½ tsp ground ginger
120 ml/4 fl oz cold water
7.5 cm/3 in cinnamon stick, broken into pieces

5 ml/1 tsp vanilla essence
900 ml/1½ pts milk
marshmallows or whipped cream for decoration

In a saucepan, combine sugar, cocoa powder, nutmeg, cloves and ginger. Gradually stir in water until mixture is smooth. Add cinnamon pieces and bring to the boil, stirring constantly. Cook 1 minute longer, stirring constantly.

Gradually beat in milk and bring mixture to below the boil, do not boil, beating constantly until mixture is

frothy. Remove from heat, beat in vanilla and strain into large cups or mugs. Top each with a few marshmallows or a dollop of whipped cream.

SWEET SUCCESS

For Minty Hot Chocolate, prepare as above but omit the nutmeg, cloves, ginger, cinnamon and vanilla. After milk is beaten in, beat in 30 ml/2 tbsp mint-flavoured liqueur or 15 ml/1 tbsp peppermint essence.

VELVETY HOT CHOCOLATE

2 SERVINGS

This is the type of hot chocolate served in the tea rooms of Paris and Vienna. A small pitcher of thick hot, melted chocolate is brought to the table with another pitcher of milk. You dilute the chocolate to taste; then add a little whipped cream — it is heavenly.

100 g/4 oz plain chocolate, chopped
45 ml/3 tbsp cold water
30 ml/2 tbsp hot water
475 ml/16 fl oz milk
whipped cream for decoration

In the top of a double boiler over low heat, melt chocolate and cold water, stirring frequently until smooth. Remove from heat and beat in hot water, beating until smooth. Pour into a small pitcher or 2 large cups or mugs.

In a saucepan, bring milk to the boil and pour into a separate pitcher, or pour some of the milk into each cup or mug of chocolate. Top with whipped cream and serve immediately.

RICH ICED CHOCOLATE

`MAKES 2 TALL DRINKS`

This is a wonderful summertime drink: a rich combination of creamy chocolate and espresso coffee served in a tall glass over crushed ice.

250 ml/8 fl oz whipping cream
100 g/4 oz plain chocolate, chopped
10 ml/2 tsp vanilla essence
475 ml/16 fl oz freshly brewed espresso coffee, chilled
sugar to taste
grated chocolate for decoration (optional)

In a small saucepan over medium heat, bring cream to the boil. Add chocolate all at once, stirring until smooth. Remove from heat and stir in vanilla. Strain into a bowl. Cool to room temperature. Refrigerate about 1 hour to chill but do not allow chocolate to "set."

To serve, beat cold espresso into the chilled chocolate until well blended and frothy. Fill 2 tall glasses one-quarter full with crushed ice, then pour chocolate-coffee mixture over. Sprinkle with grated chocolate.

`SWEET SUCCESS`

If you prefer sweetened coffee, add sugar to taste to espresso mixture while it is still hot to be sure sugar is well dissolved.

DRINKS

EXTRA-CHOCOLATE MILK SHAKE

2 SERVINGS

Everyone has their own version or favourite chocolate milk shake — try this for a real chocolate treat.

50 g/2 oz cocoa powder
100 g/4 oz sugar
120 ml/4 fl oz water
75 ml/2½ fl oz golden syrup
5 ml/1 tsp vanilla essence
120 ml/4 fl oz cold milk
15 ml/1 tbsp chocolate-flavoured
  liqueur

300 ml/10 fl oz chocolate ice cream
grated chocolate

First make the chocolate syrup. In a saucepan over medium heat, combine cocoa and sugar. Gradually stir in water until smooth and well blended. Stir in golden syrup, then bring to the boil, stirring frequently.

Cook 2–3 minutes, stirring constantly until mixture is smooth and thickened. Remove from heat and stir in vanilla.

Cool slightly.

In a blender or milk-shake machine, combine milk, chocolate syrup and liqueur (if using). Blend 30 seconds. Add ice cream and blend about 45 seconds, just until smooth. Pour into 2 tall glasses and decorate with chocolate curls or grated chocolate.

CHOCOLATE CREAM LIQUEUR

MAKES ABOUT 1.1 L/2 PTS

This creamy, smooth after-dinner drink is surprisingly easy to make.

15 ml/1 tbsp instant espresso or coffee
  powder
25 g/1 oz cocoa powder
250 ml/8 fl oz milk
250 ml/8 fl oz double cream
400 g/14 oz can condensed milk
1 egg yolk
250 ml/8 fl oz whisky
75 ml/2½ fl oz light rum
15 ml/1 tbsp vanilla essence
15 ml/1 tbsp coconut essence

In a large, heavy-bottomed saucepan, combine espresso and cocoa powders. Gradually stir in milk until powders are dissolved. Stir in cream and condensed milk and bring to the boil.

In a bowl, lightly beat egg yolk. Pour about 250 ml/8 fl oz hot cream mixture over egg yolk, beating well, then stir cream-and-egg mixture back into the pan. Cook 2–3 minutes longer until mixture thickens and coats the back of a spoon. Remove from heat. Stir in whisky, rum and vanilla and coconut

essences. Strain into a bowl and cool to room temperature, stirring occasionally. Refrigerate 2–3 hours until well chilled.

Transfer to a bottle or jar with a tight-fitting lid and store in the refrigerator. Shake before serving.

DELUXE CHOCOLATE EGG NOG

10–12 SERVINGS

This drink is made with raw egg and should be kept refrigerated.

250 g/9 oz plain chocolate, chopped
475 ml/16 fl oz milk
6 eggs
50 g/2 oz sugar
120 ml/4 fl oz brandy or rum
120 ml/4 fl oz Amaretto liqueur
30 ml/2 tbsp vanilla essence
475 ml/16 fl oz whipping cream
grated chocolate or cocoa powder for
  decoration

In a saucepan over low heat, melt chocolate and 250 ml/8 fl oz milk, stirring frequently until smooth. Remove from heat and stir in remaining cold milk until well blended. Cool to room temperature.

With electric mixer, beat eggs and sugar until pale and thick, 5–7 minutes. Gradually beat in cooled chocolate, liqueurs and vanilla.

In another bowl with hand-held electric mixer, beat whipping cream just until soft peaks form. Stir a spoonful of

cream into chocolate-egg mixture then fold in remaining cream. Chill.

SWEET SUCCESS

To prepare without alcohol, omit the brandy and liqueur and substitute 250 ml/8 fl oz milk, chocolate milk or cream.

FROM TOP, CLOCKWISE: EXTRA-CHOCOLATE MILK SHAKE, CHOCOLATE CREME LIQUER, AND DELUXE CHOCOLATE EGG NOG ▶

INDEX